Alain Dag' Naud

Wonderful
LANGUEDOC-
ROUSSILLON

Photographs by:
Catherine Bibollet

Catherine Bibollet is represented by TOP-RAPHO, Paris

Translated by:
Angela Moyon

ÉDITIONS OUEST-FRANCE
13, rue du Breil, Rennes

Summary

A land of rocks and fire

The Gévaudan area was famous for its wild beast, a monstrous wolf with a taste for human flesh. In days gone by in Narbonne, there lived a maid who was as beautiful as day but who was also a witch and a vampire; she turned her husband into a dog. There are hidden treasures everywhere, some buried by the Saracens and the Knights Templar, others including the dragon's garnet and why not the Holy Grail itself? The swallowholes that pit the Causse area are like entrances to Hell. The caves are the home of the Little People. Dolmens and phantom towers stand guard on outcrops of rock. The Cathar fortresses soar beyond the skyline, communicating through an enigmatic sort of geography of the zodiac. This is the Languedoc and the

Lozère. Caves in the Saint-Chély corrie.

A land of rocks and fire

Ariège. The Cathar castle of Roquefixade.

Roussillon, regions where mystery reigns, where legends go hand-in-hand with history, and where extraordinary events seem to be everyday occurrences.

Even nature is larger than life. On the southernmost ridge of the Massif Central, rivers gouge out devils' cauldrons. The Tarn, Jonte and Dourbie roar through their gorges. Rushing waters cascade down over the cliffs. Underground mazes like Dargilan or the Aven Armand tail off into abysses. In Montpellier-le-Vieux, Mourèze, and Les Arcs de Saint-Pierre, the rocks form strange shapes, like ruined buildings. On the Grands Causses, circular dips called "lavognes" and "sotches" are veritable oases in an otherwise arid landscape. The scrub backing onto the Cévennes produces some incredibly

Rooftops in Ispagnac, Lozère.

subtle perfumes. The seemingly endless waves of vineyards on the lower slopes flutter in the slightest breeze. The lakes and Mediterranean soak up the sunshine. And over there, further south, like ramparts round Spain, stand the Pyrenees, tumbling into the sea in a frenzy of headlands and creeks.

How could anybody not love such a place, the stone-slabbed roofs of the houses, the carnal mysticism of the Romanesque churches, and the haughty nostalgia of the fortified cathedrals? How could anybody not love the sincerity, independence and fervour of the local people? In the complex rugby scrums, the nautical jousts in Agde and Sète, the circular formation of the sardane danced to the sounds of the cobla on the squares in Perpignan and Collioure, there is an ideal for life and a blend of aestheticism and unity.

The highly individualistic character of the Oc region has been strengthened three times in its history by bloody events. First of all, there was the Albigensian Crusade which began in 1226. Catharism was not representative of the

5

entire Occitan region but, here more than anywhere else, it found a refuge in an area where tolerance bore the imprint of romanity. The noblemen from the north, who used the "oïl" dialect, set off to war for the pleasure of it, did not understand the troubadours' Courts of Love, and coveted the south's riches. In the name of the Cross, Simon de Montfort committed murder and arson. By the Treaty of Paris, signed in 1229, Lower Languedoc was annexed to the kingdom. Montségur fell in 1244. Upper Languedoc was integrated in 1271 as a result of nothing more complicated than an inheritance.

The wounds began to heal and life began again. Wool and silk again provided employment, and the fairs in

Aveyron. Roquefort-sur-Soulzon.

Carcassonne and Beaucaire exported cloth, woad and wine. The universities in Toulouse and Montpellier flourished. Yet the feeling of independence and the taste for subversive ideas still remained. When, in 1536, tradesmen from Geneva began to speak of Protestantism, they

were well-received. There were numerous converts in the Cévennes, the Montagne Noire and the Vivarais. For forty years, Catholic bands led by Joyeuse or Montluc confronted the members of the Reformed Religion led by the Baron des Adrets or the Duke de Montmorency. The Edict of Nantes (1598) calmed spirits slightly. Its stupid revocation in 1685 rekindled all the old hatreds. Louis XIV's dragoons pillaged and raped with impunity. In 1702, the Camisard (literally "shirt-sleeve") revolt broke out. It was put down with a terrifying cruelty that was never to be forgotten. Even today, in the villages of the Cévennes, Protestants and Catholics have little to do with each other. Mixed marriages are rare. The cemete-

Hérault. Lake Salagou

ries are divided in two. Politically, the Protestant farmers believe themselves to be more leftwing than their Catholic counterparts.

The last drama was caused by the vineyards. Languedoc and Roussillon are both wine-growing regions, as shown by produce such as Muscat, Grenache, Banyuls, Maury, Rivesaltes, Côtes-du-Roussillon, Coteaux-du-Languedoc, Minervois, Corbières, the sparkling Blanquette de Limoux etc. In the early years of the 20th Century, pro-

duction far exceeded demand and prices dropped sharply. In 1907, the winegrowers revolted. From Paris, Clémenceau ordered repressive measures. But the soldiers in the 17th Infantry Regiment, all of them local people by birth, refused to fire on the demonstrators. The worst was avoided.

Through sword and fire, for justice and truth, Languedoc and Roussillon were regions where revolt was widespread. Its people, men and women alike, all with unsubmissive hearts, either gave of their all or refused it totally. There were no half measures. This was what gave their character its beauty, just like the landscape

Pyrénées-Orientales. The Mystery of the Incarnation, a fresco in the chapel in Saint-Martin-de-Fenollar.

with its impressive scenery full of stones and rocks, its deserts dotted with oases, and the sea that is ever fresh and new. For you, the visitor in search of something, or even something else, elsewhere, Languedoc and Roussillon are there, waiting for you to begin your quest.

Hérault. Saint-Martin-de-Londres.

Aude. Carcassonne. The town, the archaeology museum, and a round "Cathar" gravestone.

Glimpses of Languedoc and Roussillon

THE FIVE DEPARTMENTS

Aude (11) - *Main town:* Carcassonne
Sub-préfectures:
Narbonne, Limoux

Gard (30) - *Main town:* Nîmes
Sub-préfectures: Alès,
Le Vigan

Hérault (34) - *Main town:* Montpellier
Sub-préfectures: Béziers,
Lodève

Lozère (48) - *Main town:* Mende
Sub-préfecture: Florac

Pyrénées-Orientales (66)
Main town: Perpignan
Sub-préfectures: Céret,
Prades

THE LONGEST BEACH IN FRANCE

From Camargue to Pyrenees, from the Petit Rhône to Cap Cerbère, the coastline flanking the Golfe du Lion unfurls an almost unbroken line of sandy beaches. Property development was unknown in this area until the 1960's. Le Grau-du-Roi, La Grande Motte, Palavas-les-Flots, Cap d'Agde, Sérignan and Valras Plage, Port-la-Nouvelle, Port-Leucate, Canet, and Argelès all bear witness to the expansion of tourism in "French California". Everything in this area has some connection with water - with the Mediterranean and with the inland lakes (Thau, Mauguio, Vic, Méjean, Ingril, Bagnas to name but a few). There are 16,000 hectares of lakes and ponds dotted across the area like a string of beads, separated from the blue waters of the Mediterranean by a slender sand bar interspersed with a few lakes. The waters are ideal for bream, sea perch and elvers. Bouzigues oysters are farmed here. And pink flamingoes add a splash of brilliant colour to the scenery.

Argelès and the coast.

VINES
AND WINES

Languedoc-Roussillon has been blessed by Bacchus since the days of the Ancient Romans. The local plonk produced in large quantities in the plain is gradually giving way to high-quality wines. Towards the Rhône winegrowers produce Lirac and Tavel in the Costières and on the hillsides, Muscat in Lunel, Clairette in Bellegarde, white Picpoul in Pinet, red wine in Faugères and Muscat in Frontignan which is sold in a spiral-shaped bottle that is said to have been shaken clean by Hercules in his efforts not to waste a drop of the precious nectar. The Corbières produce Fitou and eleven other wines with a bouquet, taste and charm all of their own. Around Minerve, Muscat reigns supreme. Limoux is famous for its Blanquette. Roussillon specialises in natural sweet wines such as Banyuls, Rivesaltes and Maury, and in green wines from Bages and Collioure.

Photos CEPHAS

Wonderful Languedoc-Roussillon

*Hérault. A reconstruction of an inn,
in the museum in Béziers.*

RUGBY

South-West France is the land of rugby. Whether League or Union, this is a very physical game which develops team spirit and strength and demands an ability to dodge opponents, push forward and throw the ball backwards! Carcassonne, Pia and the XIII Catalan are the most outstanding teams in Rugby League. Béziers was, for many years, the team to beat in Rugby Union. From 1971 to 1984, AS Béziers was eleven times French champion. Over the past few years, though, the victor's shield seems to have taken up residence in the pink city of Toulouse.

LOCAL FOOD

Among the delights awaiting visitors are Langogne frogs, *Bleu de Causses* cheese, Lozère rennet, the famous Castelnaudary *cassoulet,* Narbonne-style snails, calf's head Occitan-style, larded braised veal with Quillan mushrooms, trout braised in Blanquette de Limoux, onion omelette, beef *à la gardianne, criadillas* (white bulls' kidneys), *anchoïade,* Collioure anchovies, *escuedella* (a Catalan stew), duck with olives from Saint-Jean de Fos, Sète-style *bourride* (fish soup) and countless other local dishes.

OCCITAN LANGUAGE

To counterbalance *oïl,* the language of northern France, *oc* spread throughout most of the provinces south of the R. Loire apart from the Basque country and Catalonia. The language was given its finest expression in the poems of the 12th and 13th-century troubadours. It was perpetuated in written form through authors such as the Nobel prizewinner Frédéric Mistral, one of the seven members of Félibrige, a movement which was set up in 1854 to give the Occitan language back its literary dimension.

*Hérault.
A jouster in Sète.*

JOUSTING

On the Monday nearest to August 25th, the Feast of St. Louis, impressive giants perched on the bows of large colourful boats do their utmost to throw their opponents into the water of the Royal Canal in Sète by planting the three iron spikes on their lances into the enemy's bulwarks. One of the heroes of this unusual sport was Vincent Cianni, "Hundred-Times Victor" whose carved gravestone can be seen in Sète cemetery. Other jousts are held in Mèze, Marseillan, Frontignan, Agde and Béziers.

THE "BOUVINE"

Bullfights held in the arenas in Nîmes, Béziers, Lunel, Céret etc. are traditional affairs ending with the death of the bull but some towns organise a "bouvine" instead. The centre of attention is, again, a bull but the animal is not killed. A dozen men dressed in white, called the "razeteurs" try to pull a red fabric cockade off the bull, along with the white wool tassels at the base of the horns, and two lengths of string under the tassels. This is followed by a frenzied race - and woe betide anybody who does not jump over the barrier quickly enough. Ten or more razeteurs have been killed since the last war.

*Collioure.
A Catalan fishing boat.*

Gard. A bronze statue in front of the Roman arena in Nîmes.

ANIMALS
OF LEGEND AND FANTASY

A few animals have featured in the legends or history of Languedoc. The Béziers camel was ridden by St Aphrodise; its exploits are celebrated at the end of April. The Gignac donkey saved its town by braying so loudly that it gave the townspeople plenty of warning of an impending attack by the Moors. This event is celebrated at Ascensiontide. The Montagnac goat provided miraculous milk which cured the wife of one of the aldermen. The Roujan hedgehog, which is honoured in April and again on 14th July, protected the town against attack from a monster named Tarasque. Most of all, however, there is the very real beast of Le Gévaudan, one (or more) wolves, which killed more than one hundred people between 1764 and 1766.

The Languedoc coast

AGDE, A MEDITERRANEAN GEM

Cap-d'Agde. The Ephebe in La Clape Museum.

There were very few traces of the Agathe Tyche of Antiquity left (its name meant Good Fortune) until the famous Sunday in September 1964 when the wonderful "Ephebe of Agde" was raised from the floor of the R. Hérault. It is a Greek bronze statue dating from the 4th Century B.C. After many years on show in the Louvre, it returned to the shores of the Mediterranean in the spring of 1987.

The Phocaenans and, later, the Romans had laid out a well-sheltered harbour here, in the shadow of the Mount Saint-Loup volcano, but it was pushed further inland by the alluvium deposits of the Rhône and was finally superseded by Sète. The basalt rocks of Mount Saint-Loup were used for the building of a large number of houses and St. Stephen's cathedral (Saint-Etienne) whose thick fortified walls are topped with machicolations and crenalations. The 114-foot high square tower served as a keep. The cathedral is said to have been built on the site of a temple in honour of Diana the Huntress.

There are some splendid buildings nestling in the old districts of Agde - St. Andrew's Church (Saint-André, 1525), St. Sever's Church (1499), the town hall with its loggia and arcades, the Bonaparte Fountain and the Agde

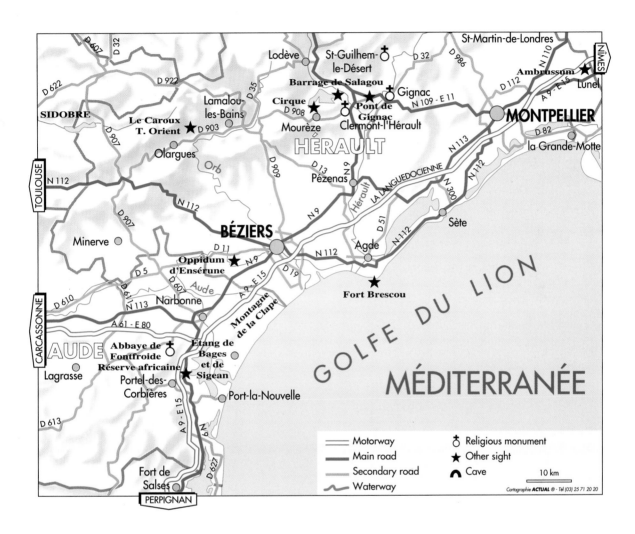

Agde. St. Stephen's Cathedral.

Museum which has extensive local history collections.

In *Besson*, the Ricard distillery is worth a visit, as is the Oyster Farming Museum in Bouzigues.

Offshore past Cap d'Agde is the Brescou Fort, which keeps watch over the metamorphosis taking place along the coast. Marinas, villas, hotels and blocks of flats have sprung up right along the coastal road on the slopes of the extinct volcano. Yet there is no concrete jungle. Mediterranean harmony has been preserved.

Wonderful Languedoc-Roussillon

AMBRUSSUM,
STEEPED IN CLASSICISM

*A*mbrussum lies just over 4 miles north-east of Lunel, within the district of Villetelle. Since the first digs were undertaken in 1967, the site has become one of the major sources of information about life in Languedoc from the 3rd millenium B.C. until the days of the Roman occupation. Situated on the Domitian Road that led from the Rhône to the Pyrenees, the hillfort of Ambrussum was used as a stopover and a refuge. All that remains of this twofold purpose is a remarkable paved road, the ruins of ramparts and towers, foundations of houses and one archway of the wonderful Ambroix Bridge. The other spans were washed away over the years when the R. Vidourle was in spate, an exceptionnally large amount of damage having occurred in 1933.

Béziers.
St. Nazaire's Cathedral.

BÉZIERS,
CENTRE OF OCCITANIAN CULTURE

*T*he horror of July 1209 hung over *Béziers* for many a long year. The entire population was massacred, whether Cathar or Roman Catholic, after the famous phrase "Kill them all. God will recognise his own!" uttered by Arnaud, the Papal legate. Seven thousand people perished in the Church of Mary Magdalen alone! Today, it is life that predominates. Doubtless the effect of the sunshine, rugby football, and the vineyards round about…

Standing high above the R. Orb and surrounding area is the old St. Nazaire's Cathedral, a fine fortified building. In the West Front is a rose window that is 32 ft. in diameter. The nave includes a few remnants of the original Romanesque church, which was burnt to the ground by Simon de Montfort.

The St. Aphrodise Basilica, which is older still, is dedicated to the town's patron saint. He was martyred in the 1st century A.D. The tomb of the holy bishop is used as a baptismal font. Its waters are said to have miraculous powers. Aphrodise' feast day, 29th April, is marked by the procession of the "camel", a colossal effigy of the animal on which Aphrodise made his entry into Béziers.

After a visit to the Museum of Old Béziers (Musée du Vieux-Biterrois) specialising in the history of the town and wine, you might like to go and meditate on the unusual pathways in Poets' Corner (Plateau des Poètes), a lovely park at the end of the Allées Paul-Riquet. Pierre-Paul de Riquet (1604-1680), who was a native of Béziers, was the famous designer of the South of France Canal lin-

Béziers, Poets' Corner.

king the Atlantic Ocean and the Mediterranean. Béziers has two of the strangest bridges across this canal — the "canal bridge" which takes the barges across the R. Orb, and the ladder that takes them up the Fonsérannes Hill.

For many years, it was wine that brought the Béziers area its wealth. In the 19th Century, a hundred or more country houses were built in the middle of the vineyards, all of them unlikely follies erected for extremely rich vineyard owners. Among the most outstanding are *Château de la Tour* (1887) which has wainscoting and a fireplace built of stone and glazed earthenware, the Château de Roueïre, the houses in Contrôle, La Jourdonne, and Libouriac, the Classical *Château de Raissac* and its greenhouses, and the *Château de Belle-Ile* whose owner invited the Scala of Milan to his vast auditorium.

Some twelve miles north-west of Béziers by the D14 is the Premonstratensian abbey of *Fontcaude* set in the depths of a valley. It has a superb Romanesque apse with half-rounded vaulting.

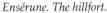

Ensérune. The hillfort.

ENSÉRUNE, A SUN-DRENCHED HILLSIDE

*E*nsérune is a hillfort 390 ft. above the plain outside Béziers. It is a particulary important position and has been occupied since the early days of Antiquity. The archaeological digs begun in 1915 showed that, in the 6th Century B.C, food was stored in silos dug into the rock. The influence of Ancient Greece led to the building of stone houses right across the hill, protected by ramparts. There was a special place for cremations. The Gauls and, later, the Romans built new fortifications, paved the streets, and created a network of sewers. Then the town entered a period of torpor in the 1st century A.D.

The archaeological finds are on show in the museum —earthenware jars (or "dolia"), Athenian cups etc. There is even an egg, unbroken after being laid in a grave more than 25 Centuries ago!

At the foot of the hill, the lie of the land forms a gigantic solar wheel. However, do not be tempted to see it as some sort of esoteric symbol. In the 13th Century, it was decided to drain the Montady Lake and our forefathers dug out lines of ditches radiating from a central collection point. From there, an underground canal took the water to the Capestang Lake.

FONTFROIDE
ABBAYE

In 1093 A.D, a handful of monks wandered across the Corbières in search of a place of prayer. In the depths of a valley full of cypress trees, arbutus and rock roses, the monks discovered a cool spring ('Fons froide'), an oasis of peace and tranquillity that was well-suited to a life of meditation. They founded a monastery there and, in 1143, it became affiliated to the Order of Cîteaux. In the Middle Ages, *Fontfroide* enjoyed enormous power. It was a bastion of orthodox Christian faith in the face of Catharism. In January 1208, the assassination of one of its brothers, Pierre de Castelnau, who had become a papal legate, was taken as a pretext for the launching of a crusade against the Albigensians. From 1311 to 1317, the abbey was ruled by Jacques Fournier, later to become Pope in 1334, under the name of Benedict XII. Then the rigours of Cistercian life began to fade beneath the abbey's opulence. Fontfroide was sold during the French Revolution, disfigured, even sold off

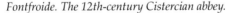

Fontfroide. The 12th-century Cistercian abbey.

Fontfroide. The guardroom in the abbey.

stone-by-stone to the Americans, and it was not until the 20th Century that it became alive once more, thanks to the care of its new owners, the Fayets.

Beyond the main courtyard, which was commissioned by the luxury-loving abbots of the 17th Century, the buildings date from the Middle Ages and are a curious blend of mysticism and earthly beauty. The Gothic cloisters are a 13th-century gem, with alterations dating from the 17th Century.

Light and shade give them a vibrant harmonious life of their own. The minster, first built in the second half of the 12th Century, is remarkable for the height of its barrel-vaulted nave. Side chapels were added in the 13th and 15th Centuries. Some of its features seem to be timeless, like the Chamber of the Deceased with its stone calvary, the chapter house, the monks' cells that marked a departure from the rule relating to communal dormitories, the 11th-century undercroft, and the wonderful Italian-style gardens. "In Fontfroide, the waters are icy cold but the hearts are warm", said Déodat de Séverac.

Fontfroide. The cloisters.

La Grande-Motte. The Frantour Hotel.

Gruissan and the lakes.

LA GRANDE-MOTTE

In the 1960's, diggers began to rip the lakes apart, and dikes and yachting marinas were built. From Argelès to the Rhône Delta, the shores of the Golfe du Lion were smothered in concrete, with a string of hotels, blocks of flats, villas, and campsites, all of them right on the water's edge, between the sea and the lakes. La Grande-Motte and Leucate formed the advance guard.

Between the Ponant Lake, the Golden Lake (Etang de l'Or) and the sea, stands *La Grande-Motte,* the town of "pyramids" designed by Jean Balladur and a team of architects. Everything has been designed with leisure in mind — yacht club, harbour, tennis courts, casino, night clubs, and restaurants. Holidaymakers can reassure themselves by remembering that the beach is not far away, just behind the eight or ten-storey buildings. And they can dream of the sandcastles of yesteryear.

GRUISSAN, 98°F IN THE MORNING

Between the sea and mountains, standing watch over the lakes, is *Gruissan,* a secretive village whose houses entwine themselves round the ruins of the ghostly Barbarossa Tower (13th Century).

A mile away between the Grazel Lake and the sea is the new resort of *Gruissan-Plage,* rows of lakeside chalets whose piles provide protection from the floods and storms that are so frequent at the equinoxes.

Overlooking the old village is la *Clape* (695 ft.), a rocky symbol of peace in the heart of the scrub. A stony path wends its way between the cypress trees and broom bushes, forming a graveyard with no dead bodies in it, simply rows of stones in memory of sailors lost at sea. At the summit, built above a cave-hermitage, stands the chapel of Our Lady of Les Auzils, or Our Lady of Assistance, the chapel used by Gruissan's seamen.

On the south bank of the *Sigean* lake is an African safari park, more than one hundred hectares in which wild animals such as antelope, rhinoceros, alligators and pink flamingoes can wander at will.

The resort of *Port-la-Nouvelle* was founded in July 1844 by Louis-Philippe. The Jugne Estate contains the impressive skeleton of a whale which was washed up on the beach in November 1989. Nearby is the largest wind-powered farm-

Gruissan.

stead in France, built in 1993. It has five gigantic windmills, 127 ft. high.

On the other side of the A9 motorway is *Portel-des-Corbières.* Some 260 ft. beneath the surface of the Corbières hills, in galleries where the wines from the Rocbère cellars are left to mature, there is a Gallo-Roman villa with paved passageways, an atrium, baths and a fountain. The villa has been entirely rebuilt in the heart of an underground chamber made of gypsum.

LAGRASSE ABBAYE

Lagrasse Abbey. The 18th-century cloisters.

A general view of Lagrasse.

On the banks of the R. Orbieu spanned by a mediaeval bridge stands the old fortified hilltop village of *Lagrasse*, which is famous for its Benedictine Abbey dating from 778 A.D. Nothing remains of the Carolingian Era except altar tablets and the base of the North tower. The buildings still standing today were erected between the 10th and 18th Centuries. Note the primitive 11th-century chapel, the church and St. Bartholomew's Chapel (late 13th Century), the fine Guardroom (15th Century), the massive belltower commissioned by Abbot Philippe de Lévis (1502-1537), the great staircase, the Abbot's Palace and the cloisters (1745-1760).

MAGUELONE, CATHEDRAL OF THE POPES

Maguelonde the Solitary, is a moving and unexpected sight, emerging as it does from the lagoons. The Melgueil lake provides protection for this tiny island with a great destiny which was inhabited in the early days of Antiquity. As the region's spiritual centre, and a bishopric from the 6th to the 8th and again from the 11th to the 16th Centuries, Maguelone had a prestigious history. The cathedral built by Bishop Arnaud from 1030 onwards was extended and embellished until 1178 and is a masterpiece of Languedoc Romanesque architecture. An outer wall protected it against possible invasion and a number of Popes sought refuge there in the 12th Century. However, in 1536, the episcopal see was transferred to Montpellier. In 1632, Richelieu ordered the demolition of the fortifications. The bridge linking Maguelone to the mainland collapsed into the waters of the lake. And Maguelone fell into a decline.

The last surviving witness of this prestigious past, the old cathedral, was saved from ruin by Frédéric Fabrège (second half of the 19th Century). Despite the removal of its crenelations on Richelieu's orders, the building has maintained a fortified appearance with mighty piers, slit-windows and the North Tower, known as the Holy Sepulchre Tower. The admirable main door has a marble tympanum depicting Christ giving His blessing. The lintel, which was hewn out of a Roman military milestone made of grey marble, is decorated with foliage. It bears a Latin inscription dated 1178. It can be translated as meaning "Come to this haven of life, all you who are thirsty. As you pass through these doors, be born again. Pray when you enter this place, and weep for your sins. Whatever your fault, it will be washed away by tears". On each side of the doorway is a bas-relief representing St. Paul *(left)* and St. Peter *(right)*.

Maguelone. The old cathedral church.

The cathedral in the centre of the lagoon.

The interior combines the austerity of a place of meditation with the skilful harmony of a well-proportioned building. The first two spans in the nave are divided by a gallery originally reserved for the canons. It partly hides the formidable ribbed arches that support the barrel vaulting built by Jean de Montlaur. On south side of the nave is St. Augustine's Chapel, all that remains of the cathedral built on Bishop Arnaud's orders in 1030. The semicircular apse is flanked by two apsidal chapels hewn into the thickness of the wall. The north crossing, or Holy Sepulchre Chapel, contains a 6th-century marble tomb known as the Tomb of Beautiful Maguelone. The Lady Chapel in the south crossing is lit by a tall Romanesque window. The walled-up doorway used to lead to the graveyard. Near the mediaeval tombs in front of the Romanesque altar is the grave of Frédéric Fabrèges (d. 1915), the saviour of Maguelone.

An 18th-century water tower on Promenade du Peyrou.

MONTPELLIER, CITY OF INTELLECTUAL PROWESS

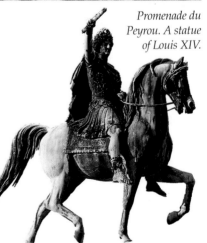

Promenade du Peyrou. A statue of Louis XIV.

The name of *Montpellier* comes from "Monspistillarius", meaning Grocers' Mount. In the 10th Century, the town was a meeting place popular with spice merchants. Later came the bankers, the pilgrims on their way to Compostella, and the doctors who wanted to learn more about the curative powers of spices. The Faculty of Medecine was founded in the 12th-13th Centuries. Since then, its renown has never waned. Rabelais studied there in the 1530's. Nowadays, the student population adds to the vitality of the town that has become the regional capital.

The 18th-century St. Clement aqueduct.

Wonderful Languedoc-Roussillon

However, Montpellier owes its plethora of large buildings to its opulent middles classes. In 1688, it was to please the king that they commissioned the famous Promenade du Peyrou designed by Giral. It opens onto a triumphal arch in honour of Louis XIV and climbs up, in terraces, to a wonderful water tower in the shape of a Corinthian temple. It is fed by the waters of the R. Lez, brought by an arched aqueduct half-a-mile long and over 71 ft. high.

In order to emphasise their power, the upper middle classes built yet more luxurious mansions. First of all, there was the Jacques-Cœur Residence, just one of the premises used by the illustrious merchant in the 1400's. This was followed, in the 17th and 18th Centuries, by the Rodez-Bénavent and Saint-Côme Mansions, the Mirman Residence with its fine staircase, the Solas Mansion which has some admirable ceilings, the Montcalm, Saint-André and Jean

Deydé Residences etc. Some of them now house famous museums such as the Fabre Museum that contains works by Veronese, Zurburan, Greuze, David, Corot, Ingres, Delacroix, Courbet, Houdon etc. The Lunaret Mansion houses archaeological collections. The Varennes Residence has reproductions of everyday life in the Languedoc of the past, while the Atger Museum on the first floor of the Faculty of Medecine contains a rich collection of artists' sketches.

The triumphal arch in honour of Louis XIV.

The 18th-century Cambacérès Residence on Place Carnougue.

The second courtyard in the Stock Exchange Treasury.

The Flower Market.

Wonderful Languedoc-Roussillon

The Varennes Residence.

Those who enjoy visiting churches will be somewhat disappointed. The Wars of Religion caused enormous damage here. However, the 14th-century St. Peter's Cathedral (Saint-Pierre), which underwent restoration in the 17th and 19th Centuries, is worth a visit. The same can be said for the 17th-century Church of Notre-Dame-des-Tables.

You cannot fully appreciate the beauty and charm of Montpellier unless you are prepared to wander at will from square to square and street to street. On the Place de la Comédie, commonly nicknamed "The Egg" (l'Œuf), stands the Opera House (1888) forming a brilliant backcloth for Etienne d'Antoine's *Three Graces*. The tiny Place Saint-Ravy leads to the beautiful Palace of the Kings of Majorca. The Babotte or Pine Towers, remnants of the town's walls, serve as reminders of the Middle Ages. And there is peace and freshness aplenty in the Esplanade Gardens, or the Jardin des Plantes, the oldest botanical gardens in France, created in 1593 by Pierre Richer de Belleval. Spare a thought for botanist Pierre Magnol who worked here and

The 17th-century Mirman residence.

gave his name to the magnolia. You can also take time to meditate beneath the famous gingko biloba planted in 1795 or near the old tree nicknamed the "lovers' letter box".

Nostradamus foretold that Montpellier would lie in ruins when the Pine Tower (Tour des Pins) lost its trees. The pines have been replaced by cypress trees that are carefully tended, and new urban districts are spreading along the capricious R. Lez to the Juvénal harbour beneath the superb neo-Classical buildings designed by Ricardo Bofill.

The Three Graces Fountain on Place de la Comédie.

The esplanade on Place de la Comédie.

Rue du Bras-de-Fer.

In the 17th and 18th Centuries, the people of Montpellier peppered the nearby countryside with "follies" and country houses. The most beautiful are *Flaugergues, La Mogère, Château d'O, l'Engarran,* and *Assas.* Further away is the magnificent Classical castle of *Castrie* and the equally attractive *Villevieille* above the picturesque fortified village of *Sommières.*

Château de Flaugergues, a 17th-century folly.

Narbonne. The Archbishops' Palace.

NARBONNE, ANCIENT ROMAN CITY

Founded in 118 B.C, Narbo Martius, now *Narbonne,* was for many years the capital of the Roman Narbonnaise province which covered nearly all of southern Gaul. After being an economic metropolis on the route between Italy and Spain, the home of the Visigoth monarchs, the seat of an archbishopric, and the fief of the Counts of Toulouse, Narbonne fell into a decline when its harbour began to silt up and the main trade routes followed the Rhône Valley and the cols across the Alps. Since last century, vineyards have brought business back to the town.

Nothing now remains of the old Roman buildings. They were demolished on the orders of François I so that their stones could be used in the building of the town walls. But Narbonne does have some very fine

mediaeval buildings, of which the most outstanding is the astonishing and grandiose cathedral of St. Just. Building work began in 1272 at the invitation of Pope Clement IV, a former Archbishop of Narbonne, and today it would have been one of the largest cathedrals in the western world if the town councillors had not opposed the demolition of the ramparts. Because of this, only

The 13th-century Gilles Aycelin Keep in the Archbishops' Palace.

The former Carmelite convent.

Horreum, a Roman warehouse.

The Chamber of the World of the Deceased.

the chancel was ever built. Its tall Gothic vaulting rises to over 133 ft. The flying buttresses rise to form turrets, balustrades have been replaced by crenelations, and two mighty square towers support the West Front. The cathedral, then, was an integral part of the town's system of defence.

St. Just contains some exceptional furnishings — a carved wooden organ, tapestries, paintings, a 14th-century alabaster statue of the Virgin Mary and several tombs at the end of the chancel. Beneath the Chapel of the Annunciation is the Treasure House containing precious incense-burners, ivories dating from the 10th and 11th Centuries, illuminated manuscripts and a 15th-century Flemish tapestry representing the Creation.

The cloisters on the south side of the cathedral originally linked it to the archbishops' palace. A few steps lead to the *Passage de l'Ancre,* a fortified street running between the old 12th-century bishop's palace and the south side. Both palaces have fine inner courtyards, galleries and sumptuous chambers that were once the apartments of the archbishops. Now they house the Archaeology Museum and the Museum of Art and History. On the former Place aux Herbes, the façade is dominated by three massive towers. Viollet-

The Art Gallery and Museum in the Archbishops' Palace.

le-Duc succeeded in finding a place for the town hall between the Gilles-Aycelin keep (13th Century) and the St. Martial Tower.

Across the R. Robine stands St. Paul's Basilica, built in 1229. It is unusual for the boldness of its vaulting and pillars. This is the town's second spiritual centre and was originally a graveyard containing the graves of Bishop Paul and the first Christians. A Paleo-Christian crypt has been uncovered, containing a number of stone coffins.

Anybody with an interest in old buildings would enjoy a visit

The Creation of the World, a 16th-century Flemish tapestry.

to the archaeological museum, which has one of the most extensive collections anywhere in the world. Housed in a disused church, it has stone coffins, carved capitals, steles, and blocks from old ramparts. Also worth a visit are the Merchant's Bridge across the Robine and the House of the Three Nursemaids (*Maison des Trois Nourrices*) which has some buxom 15th-century caryatids. It said that Cinq-Mars was arrested here after the failure of his plot to overthrow Richelieu.

Charles Trénet, who was born in the town, bears out our opinion in his song, "Faithful! I've stayed faithful... to Narbonne, my friend."

A stroll through Narbonne.

PÉZENAS, THE CONTIS' BRIGHTEST GEM

*P*ézenas, which was listed as a "town of special architectural interest" in 1950, is called the "Versailles of Languedoc". It has retained an outstanding collection of buildings from its glorious past. The cloth fairs held in the 13th Century provided enormous wealth for the local bourgeoisie. The States of Languedoc met in Pézenas between 1456 and 1692, bringing in public sector employees and noblemen who owed their rank to the administrative or legal positions that they or their ancestors had purchased. The governors, first the Montmorencys and later the Contis, wanted to turn the town into something resembling a regional capital. Molière, "actor to His Highness the Prince de Conti", lived in the house of Gély the barber. His plays, performed in 1650, 1653, and 1655-56 in the Grange-des-Prés, marked a high point in Pézenac's history. The town, though, was given to revolt and the monarchy mistrusted it. Its privileges were withdrawn and it slowly fell into a decline that lasted throughout the 18th Century.

Pézenas on market day.

Pézenas has a discreet sort of beauty. You have to open the doors of the old mansions to see the princely luxury they contain. At 8 Rue

The 15th-century staircase in the Lacoste Residence.

François Oustrin, there is the residence of the Barons-de-Lacoste (15th-17th Centuries). On Place Gambetta, once the Corn Market, there is a 17th-century shop that belonged to the barber, Gély, and the Consular House where the States of Languedoc used to meet. A few yards away is the Vulliod-Saint-Germain Museum filled with tapestries, pottery, antique furniture, and sculptures. Rue Béranger and Rue Montmorency run along the remains of the mediaeval ramparts. In Rue Sabatier, note the 18th-century workhouse; Rue de la Foire contains the 16th-century Wicques Residence and the Carrion-Nizas Mansion (16th-17th Centuries). The collegiate church of St. John in Rue Saint-Jean was designed by J-B. Franque (1740). Beside it stands the 16th-century sacristy of the White Penitents, while opposite the collegiate church is the residence of the Commanders of the Order of St. John of Jerusalem dating from the 17th Century. Out of a hundred mansions, let us just mention the Conti Residence, the Alfonce Mansion with its loggias, the Bat-d'Argent Hostelry, the Malibran Mansion, the Epine Residence, the Pastre Mansion, the Grasset Mansion etc. You will be able to enjoy a stroll that takes you past them all if you follow the itinerary drawn up by the Tourist Office. And don't leave the town without taking a look at the dark ghetto formed by Rue Juiverie and Rue des Litanies that have remanied unchanged since the 14th Century.

From Pézenas, you can visit the priory in *Cassan*, a fine example of Classical architecture, and *Valmagne Abbey*, the "cathedral in the vineyards" founded in 1138.

SALSES
THE IMPREGNABLE FORTRESS

*S*alses once controlled the border between France and Spain. In 1497, an engineer from Aragon named Ramirez had a redoubtable fortress built there, designed to withstand artillery fire. The gigantic stone and brick walls dig deep into the ground, in the very heart of the plain covered in vineyards. The rectangular fort

The main entrance to the fortress.

The north-east lookout tower.

(374 ft. long and 293 ft. wide) is surrounded by a moat 39 to 49 ft. wide and 23 ft. deep. The ramparts are 39 ft. thick. At the four corners are towers with cannon emplacements. Advance bastions control all the entrances. The keep used to be 114 ft. high but it was altered by Viollet-le-Duc who took it back to 82 ft. The stables could cater for up to three hundred horses. The accommodation beneath the parapet walkway was designed for a garrison of one thousand men.

A general view of Sète with the old town, canal and harbour.

SÈTE
AND ITS MARITIME
CEMETERY

Like all the people of Sète, the singer and songwriter Georges Brassens spent most of his childhood swimming in the Mediterranean. Like the poet Valéry, he loved the maritime cemetery from which the sea looked like a roof,

That tranquil roof where doves [strut,

Throbs between the pines, bet-ween [the graves;

Midday the Just turns into dazz-ling [flame

The ever-changing sea.

  (Paul Valéry, *Charmes*, 1922).

Other famous children of the town include the guitarist Manitas de Plata and Yvette Labrousse who became the Begum after her marriage to the Aga Khan in 1944.

Originally, *Sète* was an island culminating in Mount Saint-Clair. Two sandspits connected it to the mainland. In the 19th Century, the 52 arches of the La Peyrade Bridge linked it to Frontignan. The work on the old harbour, commissioned by Louis XIV in 1666, was completed in 1669 by Pierre-Paul Riquet. The creation of the Orsetti Basin in 1950 and the seaport in

39

Sète. The jousts on the canal.

the late 60's turned Sète into one of the largest harbours in France.

Gone are the days when the trawlers, wine tankers and salt-carrying vessels used to tie up in the heart of the town. The old harbour has been taken over by pleasure craft. Yet the waterfront and old districts round about still have a lingering flavour of their own, a blend of the smell of fish, bright colours, and joie de vivre. In August, the basin is the setting for the jousts that traditionally oppose two districts of the town — Bordigne and Môle.

The maritime cemetery high above the coastal promenade and the Saint-Louis breakwater contains Valéry's grave. Nearby, the Paul Valéry Museum includes numerous documents on the history of Sète as well as memorabilia of the poet who was born on 30th October 1871 at 65 de la Grande Rue.

Balaruc to the north is a spa town that has been famous since the days of the Ancient Romans. Madame de Sévigné's son-in-law came here to seek treatment for gout and marine mud is still very successful in relieving rheumatic pain.

The coast road (or "Corniche") leads to *Mont Saint-Clair,* a hill 569 ft. high topped by an observation platform from which there is an unforgettable view of Sète, the Thau Lake and its oyster parks, the Cévennes, and even the Pyrenees. Yet the hill provides more than a panoramic view; it is dedicated to St. Clare, protector of the blind, and to Our Lady of La Salette. Their feast days are 19th September and 19th October.

Roussillon,
a land of secrets

ARIÈGE
AND THE CATHARS

Château de Montségur.

Standing on an outcrop of rock 3,952 ft. high, *Montségur* is the symbol of Cathar resistance. On the morning of 16th March 1244, 205 "heretics", among them 50 "perfects", left the castle, processed down to the "Champ des Crémats" singing all the way, and huddled serenely together on the gigantic fire. The flames of this collective martyrdom marked the horrible end of the crusade and its massacres.

Montségur is a mystery. The citadel was built in the early 13th Century for a Cathar community. It stands well away from any place of strategic or commercial interest and has no real value in defence terms. Was it, then, a temple with secret architecture, whose walls in the form of a pentagon established a link between earthly forces and the zodiac? Was it the tabernacle of the Holy Grail, the sacred, and probably spiritual, treasure? Did the "Gate of Mankind" to the

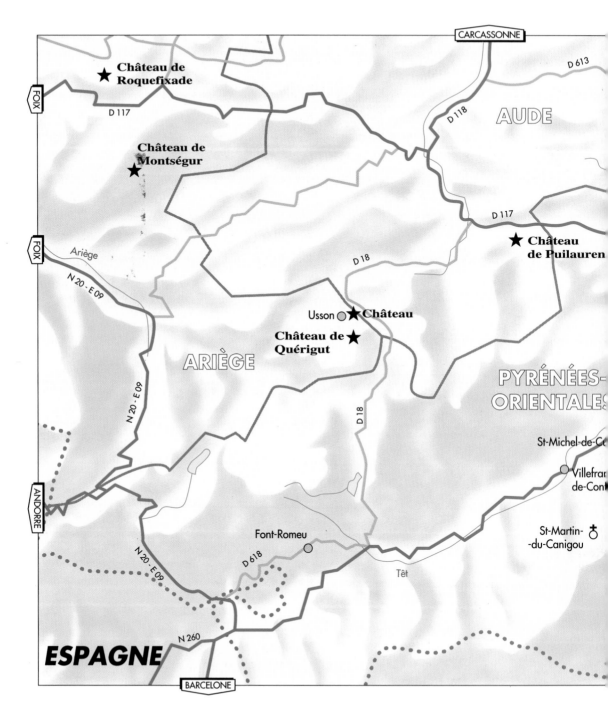

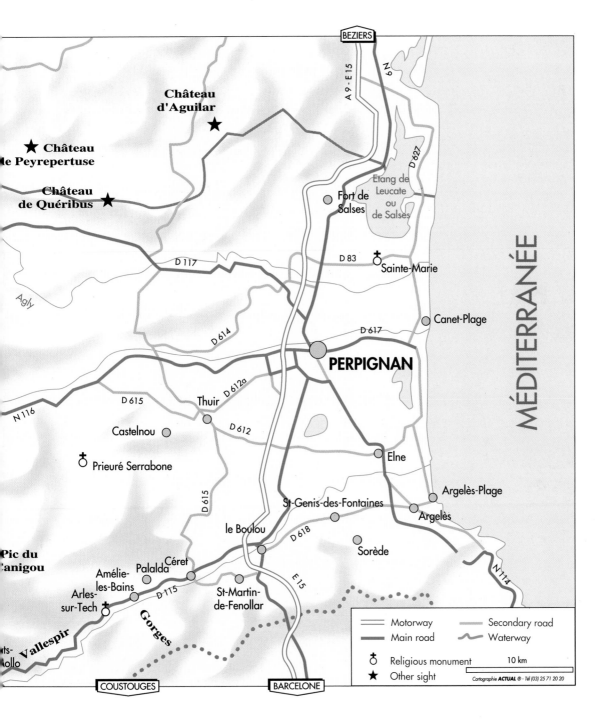

BEZIERS

A 9 - E 15

N 9

Château
d'Aguilar ★

★ Château
de Peyrepertuse

Château
de Quéribus ★

D 627

Étang de
Leucate
ou
de Salses

Fort de
Salses

D 117

D 83

⚲ Sainte-Marie

Agly

D 614

D 617

Canet-Plage

PERPIGNAN

MÉDITERRANÉE

N 116

D 615

D 612a

Thuir

D 612

Castelnou

⚲ Prieuré Serrabone

Elne

D 615

Argelès-Plage

St-Genis-des-Fontaines

Argelès

le Boulou

D 618

Sorède

Pic du
Canigou

Céret

Palalda

Amélie-
les-Bains

Arles-
sur-Tech

D 115

E 15

St-Martin-
de-Fenollar

N 114

Vallespir

Gorges

ts-
Mollo

COUSTOUGES

BARCELONE

| Motorway | Secondary road |
| Main road | Waterway |

⚲ Religious monument   10 km

★ Other sight

Cartographie ACTUAL ® - Tél (03) 25 71 20 20

Wonderful Languedoc-Roussillon

west and the "Gate of the Gods" to the north-east mark man's passage to divinity? The only evidence is the climb, sometimes a difficult affair, and it takes on all the significance of an initiation ceremony when, among all the surrounding peaks, St. Barthélemy suddenly becomes visible to the south and the heights of Roquefixade to the north-west.

Roquefixade, at the very top of a limestone ridge with a heady sheer cliff, is also an initiatory citadel but its defensive role is more marked than Montségur's.

Montségur village seen from the castle.

The great chamber in the castle, of which only the north wall remains, stood astride a gigantic crack in the rock. Hence the name of Roquefixade, i.e. "cracked rock".

UPPER AUDE VALLEY

The R. Aude flows through wooded mountains and wild isolated areas impregnated with a nobility all their own. There is the windswept *Capcir,* and the *Donezan* whose inhabitants were famous for their rebellious spirit. Our first stop, though, must be in the heart of the Donezan, at *Quérigut,* a 12th-13th century castle on a mass of fallen rock.

Quérigut. The castle and village.

Usson. The castle ruins.

In 1827 local woodcutters nicknamed "Damzels" revolted against royal authority when there was an attempt to constrain their activity. In 1848, the population set up the Independent Republic of Quérigut.

A few miles away, at the confluence of the rivers Aude and Bruyante, wrapped in the sulphurous fumes of the local springs, stand the ruins of the castle of Son, which became known as Usson in the 18th Century. It clings onto a fantastic spur of rock and is said to have been the final hiding place of the treasure of the Cathar sect. At the very gates of *Usson,* the Aude Valley narrows to a confined gorge with sheer walls of rock to each side. In the Saint-Georges Canyon, the wall of rock is more than 325 ft. high. In the *Pierre-Lys Gorge,* the road and railway follow the narrow passage gouged out by the rushing waters of the river for almost two miles until it finally flows out in the Quillan basin.

CASTELNOU

The village of *Castelnou,* near Thuir and the cellars where Byrrh is made, is a wonderful example of a fortified village sleeping peacefully behind its ramparts. At the foot of the castle of the Viscounts of Castelnou, nothing seems to have changed since the end of the 10th Century — narrow streets, old houses and town walls.

For those in search of the unusual, the Majorca Hill to the south-east is topped by the ruins of a square 12th-century keep. Because of a strange acoustic phenomenon, anything said in Majorca can be heard in Castelnou.

(bottom, left)
Castelnou. The fortified gateway.

Collioure. The Church of Our Lady of the Angels in the Mouré district.

COLLIOURE
AND THE FAUVISTS

People here live with "one foot in their vineyard and one foot in their boat". The two harbours in *Collioure*, the Cauco Illiberis of Antiquity, are filled with anchovy smacks. The Albères that form the hinterland are the last outcrops of the Pyrenees and are covered with the vineyards of Banyuls.

Picasso, Matisse, Derain and many other artists fell in love with the now-famous scenery of the tiny St. Vincent Island and beach with its 17th-century church adjacent to a Moorish tower with a pink dome that originally served as a belltower.

Wonderful Languedoc-Roussillon

In the church, the artists were fascinated by the famous Baroque reredos by Joseph Sunyer (1702). They also liked the 12th-century Knights Templars' castle that was turned into a summer residence by the Kings of Majorca and, later, fortified by Vauban.

It is a splendid setting. Yet there are those who prefer the old Mouré District. It is less of a tourist attraction but it has some pretty little alleyways and there are schist steps running across the rooftops.

Good walkers can go on a pilgrimage to the chapel of *Our Lady of Consolation* further inland, or even go as far as the

The village, church and castle.

Madeloc Tower that once kept watch over a coastline infested with Barbary pirates. From up there, creeks and headlands look like slashes in the deep blue of the Mediterranean.

Unfortunately, there are no coastal paths from Collioure so visitors have to go to *Port-Vendres* by car. This was once the "Port of Venus", given a definite sex with a white and red marble obelisk 81 ft. high. From there, follow the *Vermilion Coast* past *Cap Béar*, Banyuls, *Cap de l'Abeille*, and on to *Cap Cerbère*, the last harbour in France before the Spanish border.

Catalan fishing boats and the castle.

Puilaurens.

CATHAR FORTRESSES IN LES CORBIÈRES

*P*uilaurens was the home of Guillaume de Puylaurens, sworn enemy of Simon de Montfort. The impregnable fortress resisted attack by French forces until 1255. Turned into a royal citadel, Puilaurens then stood guard on the border with Spain. The only entrance to the castle, on the south side, was protected by staggered walls running on either side of a winding, narrow path. The square keep dates from the 11th Century. The outer walls were extended and strengthened in the 12th and 13th Centuries. In the foundations of the keep, a tunnel dug through the rock itself leads to the foot of the scarp slope to the west.

Blending into the rock on which it stands, *Peyrepertuse* is the largest Cathar fortress in the south of France. A steep but passable pathway leads up to it from Duilhac. The real difficulties begin within the multiple castle itself for there are three buildings, one above the other, dating from the 11th to 13th Centuries. Visitors who dare to climb the rocky steps of "St. Louis' ladder" and the narrow cornice over the gate will discover some fascinating mediaeval chambers whose slit windows face the direction of the sunrise at the summer solstice.

Quéribus.

Peyrepertuse.

The castle of *Aguilar,* one of the "five sons of Carcassonne" is perched on a hilltop. It consists of a vast outer wall with six towers and a polygonal keep.

Quéribus was the last centre of Cathar resistance. It fell in 1255. Its ethereal ruins stand at the very top of an outcrop of rock in the Corbières, over 2,110 ft. above Maury. The amazing square "Gothic chamber" in the polygonal keep continues to intrigue historians. The central pillar which fans out into ribbed vaulting is actually set slightly off-centre. On every hour, its shadow falls across a window, marking a position of the zodiac.

ELNE, A SACRED TOWN

E *lne* is a sanctuary dating from the earliest days of Antiquity. It is said that King Pyrene's daughter committed suicide here by setting fire to herself after Hercules' departure. At that time, the town was called Illiberis. It then became Castrum Helena, or Elne, by orders of Emperor Constantine, the son of St. Helen. In the 6th Century, Elne became the seat of a bishopric. Behind its ramparts, built in 1150, the town was a hive of activity and trade flourished. Elne, however, stands on the border with Spain and it became the object of rivalry first between Roussillon and Catalonia, and later between France and Spain. The town was pillaged in 1285 and its population

Elne. The cloisters with their twin columns and carvings of plants or imaginary animals.

slaughtered in the cathedral. More destruction followed in 1474 and Elne fell into a decline. On 30th June 1602, the Bishop moved to Perpignan. Thereafter, nothing of any importance happened to disturb the village's peaceful existence.

Nothing, perhaps, except the arrival of people with a passion for art, but they are given to quiet contemplation. St. Eulalie's Cathedral fascinates them. It was built in the 11th Century. It is a basilica with no transept and its crenelated West Front is dominated by a

FONT-ROMEU

The main therapy, tourist and sports centre in Cerdagne is *Font-Romeu* (alt. 5,850 ft.). It has an outstandingly high level of amenities and was used as a training centre for European athletes prior to the Olympic Games in Mexico. It enjoys an exceptional amount of sunshine (3,000 hours/year) and, because of this, the village of *Odeillo-Font-Romeu* was selected for the construction of a gigantic solar oven, one of the most powerful in the world with the one in Phoenix in the United States. Its huge parabolic mirror concentrates the sun's energy on an electric arc.

Font-Romeu, the "fountain of the Romeu" i.e. the pilgrim, is a major spiritual centre. In 1113, near the spring that still flows beneath the paved floor of the hermitage, a bull stopped in front of a statue of the Virgin Mary. A chapel was built on the spot. It underwent alteration in

Font-Romeu. The Hermitage.

mighty square tower and a brick tower from a more recent period. Inside, the nave has semi-circular vaulting with ribbed arches. The difference in thickness between the top and base of the pillars, and the inclusion of an additional archivolt emphasise the overall impression of length. The chapels in the south aisle contain the tomb of Bishop Raymond Costa (d. 1310), an alabaster pietà dating from the 15th Century, and a painted wooden reredos dedicated to St. Michael.

The adjacent cloisters were built for the cathedral's canons.

The southern gallery, which runs along the side of the church, dates from the 12th Century; the three others date from the 13th and 14th Centuries. In the eastern gallery are three marble tombs dating from the days of the Visigoths (6th-7th Centuries). The white Céret marble crisscrossed with blue veins, the semicircular arcading, the imaginative animals carved on the capitals and pillars, and the carved brackets are all expressions of Romaneque architecture in Roussillon at its very best.

Font-Romeu. The holiday resort.

1680 and 1741. It contains a superb reredos (1707) and the Virgin Mary's "camaril" a dainty Baroque "apartment" (1712). Both were the work of the Catalan sculptor, Joseph Sunyer. The statue, which is said to work miracles, stands in a niche behind the High Altar. It is removed on 8th September every year and carried down to the church in Odeillo where it remains until the Sunday of the Holy Trinity. Throughout this time, its place in the niche is taken by an 18th-century black statue of the Virgin Mary.

Behind the chapel, a path wends its way up the hill between Stations of the Cross. It leads to a Cross from which there is a wonderful view right across the Cerdagne area.

The D618 road to Bourg-Madame runs past the amazing Targassonne Rocks, a collection of gigantic granite boulders.

Galamus Gorge.

GALAMUS GORGE

Paying little or no heed to the natural lie of the land, the *R. Agly* has hewn an abyss some 1,625 ft. deep out of the limestone outcrop of the Corbières. From Cubières to Saint-Paul-de-Fenouillet, the cliff road, dizzily supported by low stone walls, snakes its way along the rock face high above the rushing waters of the river and the waterfalls. A stop at the l'Ermitage roundabout is a "must". The path lead up to Saint-Antoine-de-Galamus, a hermitage in a cave with iridescent walls.

PERPIGNAN

Perpignan was the capital of the short-lived kingdom of Majorca (13th-14th Centuries), the second-largest town in Catalonia after Barcelona, and the largest town in Roussillon, becoming part of France in 1659, and it has all the bustle and beauty of a regional capital. Four of its buildings bear witness to its erstwhile grandeur.

St. John's Cathedral *(cathédrale Saint-Jean)* is really a sacred "complex" with several churches in one. The chapel of Our Lady of the Ravine *(Notre-Dame des Correchs)* is the oldest religious building in Perpignan. It has wonderful doorways, and its 11th-century statue of the Virgin Mary and numerous relics (e.g. the hand of St. John the Baptist) are venerated by the entire population. The Romanesque Church of Old St. John's *(Saint-Jean-Le-Vieux)* contains an ancient font dating from the days of the Visigoths. On the marble lip is an inscription reading *Unda sacris fontis necat anguis sibila sontis* ("The water of this sacred spring chokes the wheezing of the evil snake"). Old St. John's used also to house

Wonderful Languedoc-Roussillon

Perpignan. The town seen from the top of the Castillet.

the "Pious Christ", a wooden statue of the Crucified Lord thought to date from 1307. Legend has it that the head is tilting inexorably to one side. When the chin touches the chest, the end of the world will be at hand. This figure of Christ is now in a chapel adjacent to the cathedral. The cathedral itself dates from the 14th and 15th Centuries. It has a single nave that is unusually wide (42 ft. for a length of 260 ft.)

The Palace of the Kings of Majorca is a gem of vernacular Catalonian architecture. It was built in 1276 by King James II. At the back of the main courtyard is the church consisting of two chapels one above the other — St. Mary Magdalene's on the ground floor and the Holy Cross above it. The second of these chapels, a veritable architectural gem, was reserved for the sovereigns. The king lived on the first floor of the south wing : the queen lived in the north wing. The Majorca Chamber *(salle de Majorque)* was used for official receptions. On the ground floor were the larders and storerooms, the guardrooms and lodgings. Emperor Charles V had a gigantic outer wall built around the castle; it was consolidated by Vauban. The tall walls, bastions, watchtowers, and fortified gateways form a fairly austere military complex. Note St. Florine's Well, which is 130 ft. deep and which provided the castle's water supply.

The Castillet was built in 1368 by Sanche, the second King of Majorca. It was one of Perpignan's gates and a much-feared prison, yet its tall red brick walls topped by crenelations and machicolations look

The Palace of the Kings of Majorca.

The Castillet.

like a theatrical backcloth. The Castillet now houses the Casa Pairial, i.e. the Catalan Museum of Popular Arts and Crafts.

The Maritime Office *(Loge de Mer)* is the busy heart of the town. Built in 1397 and extended in the 16th Century, this wonderful example of Hispano-Moorish architecture was used as an exchange and maritime consulate. On the Place de la Loge, there is also the former Deputation Palace (1488) and the town hall (13th-15th Centuries) in which the courtyard/patio is decorated with a statue by Aristide Maillol called "Thought". These four symbolic monuments, all of them admirable, should not be allowed to exclude the 14th-century

Thought by Maillol.

Wonderful Languedoc-Roussillon

Place Arago.

Perpignan-the-wealthy.

A mediaeval pageant.

Réal Church at the foot of the citadel, the 13th and 14th-century St. James Church *(église Saint-Jacques)* whose pink brick bell-tower overlooks a mysterious garden and the plain far below, the huge Carmelite church built in 1345, or the Blackfriars' monastery that has, at long last, been restored.

Perpignan is a capital city. As you wander through it, you will come across old houses (Mediaeval Julia with its arca-ded patio, Xanxo in the Rue de la Maison-de-Fer, and the Inquisition's House in the Rue du Théâtre dating from the Renaissance). You will find unusual streets with a charm that is typically Mediterranean and shady squares where people enjoy dancing the *"sardane"* in honour of the sun-shine.

The seaside is not far away. It is only 6 miles to the beach and two museums in *Canet.* The Toy Museum has 3,400 antique games and toys; the Boat Museum has a collection of one hundred model boats.

It was in the Perpignan hinter-land, on the hillsides of the Fenouillèdes area, that the famous Tautavel Man lived 450,000 years ago. His skull was discovered in the Caune de l'Ara-go cave. The wonderful *Tautavel Museum* will teach you more about this *homo erectus* and his environment.

Planès. The church with the layout of a star-shaped polygon.

PLANÈS

If you enjoy getting your teeth into an esoteric mystery, consider the tiny church in *Planès*. There is not another one like it in the whole of Europe. Built in the 12th or 13th Century 5,200 ft. above sea level, it is shaped like an equilateral triangle flanked by a semi-circular apsidal chapel on one side and topped by a circular dome. Later alterations attempted to hide this triangular layout, which was considered as too "unusual". Was this originally a Moslem sanctuary representing one of the seals of Solomon? Or does it symbolise a star whose branches point to a number of centres of religious culture in the region, thereby creating an enigmatic form of sacred geography?

At the foot of the hamlet, the ramparts of *Mont-Louis* were designed by Vauban to stand guard over the upper Têt and Aude Valleys.

The Pyrenean road then runs along the banks of the Têt towards Conflent. Just before the Carança Gorge is the Cerdagne railway bridge, a technical feat designed by an engineer named *Séjourné*. The arch is over 97 ft. high and is topped by a pillar 114 ft. high!

ROUSSILLON THE ROMANESQUE

Saint-Martin-de-Fenollar is an apparently modest chapel. Yet it contains the most outstanding collection of frescoes in the whole of the Roussillon. On the vaulted roof, there is a painting of Christ in Majesty flanked by the four Evangelists. Also represented are the twenty-four old men of the Apocalypse, the Annunciation, the Nativity (the Virgin Mary is shown lying on a tester bed!), the Three Wise Men etc.

The neighbouring spa town of *Boulou* specialises in the treatment of liver complaints. It has a lovely church with a finely-carved doorway. From here, head for *Saint-Genis-des-Fontaines* where the Benedictines founded an abbey in the late 9th Century. It was sold off as national property in 1796 and, in 1922, was acquired by an antique dealer who dismantled the cloisters in order to sell the

Saint-Martin-de-Fenollar.
The Mystery of the Incarnation,
a fresco in the chapel.

SAINT-MARTIN-DU-CANIGOU, THE MAGNETIC PYRAMID

Perched on its eagle's nest some 3,555 ft. above sea level, the Benedictine abbey of *Saint-Martin-du-Canigou* was built from 1001 onwards by Count Guifred de Cerdagne. He retired there in 1035 and spent the last years of his life digging his own grave in the rock. The buildings fell into disrepair and lay half in ruins before being restored between 1902 and 1932 under the leadership of Mgr Carsalade du Pont, Bishop of Perpignan, and between 1952 and 1972 by Father de Chabannes.

With its local stones half-buried in mortar, and its few narrow windows, the church has a plain, almost rustic, appearance. Yet beneath its stocky exterior, Saint-Martin hides an architectural revolution, a decisive step in the birth of Romanesque architecture. This was the first French church built in the shape of a Latin cross with a stone roof over semi-circular barrel vaulting. This explains the thickness of the walls and the smallness of the nave (20 ft. high and 11 ft. wide). When the Canigou swelters in the heat of the sun, the shade and coolness of the nave are ideal for meditation.

The adjacent cloisters, of which only three galleries still remain, nestles in the heart of the rock. And was the great

columns and capitals to the Château des Ménuls near Paris and to Philadelphia in the United States of America. Fortunately, since 1993, restoration work has been undertaken and many of the stones have been remounted. The Romanesque church in the village has a carving on its lintel dating from 1020. It includes the first example of human figures in Romanesque carving. The adjacent cloisters have been dismantled. Some sections are now in the United States; others in the Louvre.

The more recent church of *Saint-André-de-Sorède* is surprisingly ornate. The tympanum and lintel have carvings that are even more full of life than the ones in Saint-Genis.

This brief excursion into the heart of Romanesque Roussillon leads us to *Argelès* and the fine beach that seems to beckon visitors to take a dip.

Saint-Martin-du-Canigou.
The Benedictine abbey

Wonderful Languedoc-Roussillon

Saint-Michel-du-Cuxa. The abbey in the heart of the Conflent area.

square belltower rising up like a lookout post designed to control the terrible telluric waves of the *Canigou?* For the granite beneath this pyramid-shaped mountain whose summit rises to 9,048 ft. contains iron and manganese. Their presence explains the series of plane crashes in the vicinity.

The Canigou caused the planes' instrument panels to malfunction, drawing the aircraft inexorably to its slopes like a magnet. There is, then, a very fine line between the mysteries that cannot be explained by present-day technology and the monsters carved on the capitals in Saint-Martin!

Saint-Michel-du-Cuxa. Pink marble capitals and columns. The reconstructed cloisters.

SAINT-MICHEL-DE-CUXA

The bluish pyramid of the Canigou forms a backcloth. All around it, the *Conflent* forms a fertile, luminous orchard. From the depths of the Leitera Valley rises a square tower bathed in golden sunlight — *Saint-Michel-de-Cuxa.*

The abbey was founded in 883 A.D. and had its moment of glory in the 10th to 12th Centuries when Guérin and Oliba were its abbots. Then it fell into

of them and sent them to the United States. In 1926, the Metropolitan Museum of Art of New York brought them together and rebuilt the cloisters on a smaller scale in Fort Tryon Park. This is the origin of the famous "Cloisters" overlooking the Hudson River. The Americans' interest in Saint-Michel-de-Cuxa alarmed the French authorities who ordered the restoration of the church and the

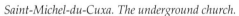

Saint-Michel-du-Cuxa. The underground church.

oblivion. In 1793, the buildings were sold off in lots and methodically dismantled by their new owners. Pillars ended up in houses nearby, capitals were taken to the public baths in Prades, and arching was transported to Aniane near Montpellier. The cloisters disappeared altogether. In 1913, the American sculptor, Georges-Guy Bernard, traced numerous sections

reconstruction of a section of the cloister galleries on their original site. Since 1965, a handful of monks have brought life back to the abbey.

Of the two square belltowers left standing at the beginning of the 19th Century, only one still exists and its four storeys and crenelations rise high into the sky. It shows the influence of the Visigoths and Mazarabs (the

Christian subjects of Moorish Spain). In the nave, curved arches rising to horseshoes resemble the vaulting in the mosque in Cordova. The crypt, called the Chapel of the Crib, was built shortly after the year one thousand by Abbot Oliba. Its circular vaulting is supported by a central pillar fanning out into ribs. For the past one thousand years, this sanctuary has welcomed pilgrims who have come to pray to the Virgin Mary of the Crib.

The cloisters were partially rebuilt, using remains discovered here and there. There are a few admirable capitals decorated with plant motifs, creatures from a fantasy world and fearsome faces. The blend of carnal and imaginative realism bears witness to the power of mysticism in the Middle Ages.

From the neighbouring town of *Prades*, birthplace of cellist Pablo Casals (1876-1973), you can visit the wonderful village of *Eus* whose old stone houses are built in tiers up the sun-drenched sides of a spur of rock facing the Canigou.

SERRABONE, BLACK SCHIST AND PINK MARBLE

On the eastern slopes of the Canigou stands the priory of *Serrabone*, a gem of Romanesque architecture. Lost amidst the silence of the Aspres and left to fall into decay for many years, the austere schist church with a square tower houses a number of treasures. In the ribbed barrel-vaulted nave are a profusion of marble pillars and capitals, brought alive by bizarre creatures, monsters, flowers and heads. The 12th-century gallery, which was originally the monks' choir, was carved out of pink marble brought from the quarries at Villefranche. The lion motif predominates throughout — lions fighting, a parade of lions, lions hunting, and the lions in the den with Daniel. Are the lions of Serrabone, which are thought possibly to have been the work of a sculptor of Jewish origin, really a homage to Christ who was the Lion of Judah?

The right arm of the transept leads to the South gallery, once the monks' promenade opening onto the mountainside. Artists, again fascinated by the Orient and Mozarabic art, were responsible for the carving.

A close-up of a capital at the entrance to the priory. (Inset) Serrabone. The Romanesque priory.

THE VALLESPIR

Palalda.

Bathed by the waters of the Tech with its frequent changes of mood, the *Vallespir* is one of the major centres of Catalan tradition and culture.

Céret, set amidst orchards of cherry, apricot and peach trees, is a haven of light filled with the trickle of fountains. Its esplanades shaded by plane trees, the daring 14th-century Devil's Bridge so called because it was thought that only the devil could have built such a thing, the 14th-century fortified gateway and the Romanesque St. Peter's Church (*église Saint-Pierre*) have all attracted artists to the town. Picasso, Braque, Dufy, Soutine, and Chagall, or again Maillol, Tristant Tzara, and Déodat de Séverac have all strolled through its streets and created works of art here. "The Mecca of Cubism" has managed to keep some of them, and they can now be seen in the Museum of Modern Art.

Further upstream, the Tech Valley narrows. *Palalda*, perched high above the river, is a pyramid of old pink-walled houses. The village is twinned with the beautiful spa town of Amélie-les-Bains which specialises in the treatment of rheumatism and respiratory disorders. The whole vicinity bristles with forests, Romanesque churches and old villages, and is crisscrossed by ravines (Mondony Gorge, Terme Gorge etc.). In fact, it seems to be beckoning visitors to go for a walk or a drive.

A few miles further on is *Arles-sur-Tech*, the religious centre of the Vallespir. Its Benedictine abbey was founded in 778 A.D. and is the oldest in Roussillon. People venerated St. Abdon and St. Sennen there, and their relics are said to have been brought to Arles by St. Arnulfe. On the left of the church door is a stone coffin from which oozes a mysterious liquid with miraculous powers. It is said that St. Arnulfe emptied the water from the coffin in which he carried the relics into this "Holy Tomb". In the church, built between the 9th and 11th

Céret.

Centuries, there is an admirable Baroque reredos (1647) representing St. Abdon and St. Sennen. The adjacent white marble cloisters date from the 13th Century.

Beyond Arles, the landscape becomes more markedly alpine. The *Fou Gorge* narrows to steep-sided passages less than 10 ft. wide crossed on footbridges. The mountain village of *Coustouges* near the Spanish border huddles round its 12th-century fortified church with two highly-ornate doorways, one beside the other.

The Romanesque church of *Serralongue* is also a beautiful building, admirable for its crenelated tower and the strap hinges on its door. Beyond the

Prats-de-Mollo.

cleft in the rocks at Baillanouse is *Prats-de-Mollo,* a picturesque little place whose 14th-century

fortifications were raised by Vauban. Walkways, watch-towers, narrow streets that are no more than flights of steps, gateways and bartizans give the citadel an atmosphere of days long gone. An impressive covered passageway leads to the Lagarde Fort above the village. The Church of St. Just and St. Rufine (17th Century) still has the crenelated Romanesque tower from the original building. At the entrance is a whalebone hung up as a votive offering. A chapel houses a copy of Notre-Dame du Coral. The original can be seen in the humble mountain shrine that is a centre of Catalan spirituality. The chapel lies above the Guille Col on the way to Lamanère.

Prats-de-Mollo. The town and its church.

EXCURSIONS IN CONFLENT

Huddling between the Canigou and the R. Têt, *Villefranche-de-Conflent* was founded in the late 11th Century by Count Guillaume-Raymond of Cerdagne. The 11th-and 15th-century ramparts were integrated into a massive system of defence by Vauban. The Queen's, King's, and Crown Prince's bastions etc. provide protection for the gates. Perched on the Belloch hill, the fort is linked to the town by an underground staircase of one thousand steps. Narrow winding alleys are flanked by rows of Romanesque houses. St. James' Church *(église Saint-Jacques)*, which stands immediately adjacent to the ramparts at the southern end of the town, was built in the early 12th Century. It has two carved doorways on the north side. Inside, people still pray to the statue of Our Lady of Success (14th Century) when epidemics are rife.

The Corneilla road leads to the *Grandes Canalettes*, a cave known familiarly as the "Underground Versailles of the Pyrenees" because of its ivory-coloured stalactites and stalagmites. Corneilla is famous for its Romanesque church. The crenelated West Front has a wonderful marble doorway (12th Century) with a carving of the Virgin Mary

Romanesque houses in Villefranche-de-Conflent.

Villefranche-de-Conflent. The France Gate in the town walls.

Wonderful Languedoc-Roussillon

Corneilla-de-Conflent. The village and the Canigou range.

in Glory on the tympanum. A Latin inscription indicates, "You who are alive, come and honour Her through whom life is given, through whom the world is born again". The plain, pure design of the apse expresses a confident spirituality. In the chancel are three Romanesque statues of the Virgin Mary seated. The marble High Altar dates from a later period.

Vernet-les-Bains on the banks of the roaring River Cady is a spa town famous for the treatment of rheumatism and ENT infections.

The famous yellow train, which was first brought into service in the early 1900's, runs between Villefranche-de-Conflent and La Tour-de-Carol. It covers a distance of 39 miles and climbs from 1,388 ft. up to an altitude of 4,313 ft. across viaducts and suspension bridges.

The spa town of Amélie-les-Bains.

Albi and Upper Languedoc

ALBI

Let's not beat about the bush — Albi is a wonderful place. Seen from the old bridge (*Pont-Vieux*) across the R. Tarn or the Pont du 22 août, the long red nave of St. Cecilia's Cathedral keeps watch like a tranquil sphynx. This brick masterpiece was first commissioned by Bernard de Castanet in 1282, shortly after the end of the Albigensian Crusade. The square belltower-keep, which was built in the 15th Century, and the tower-shaped piers marked the Church's newly-regained supremacy in a town that had been the springboard of the Cathar religion.

Before entering the cathedral, visitors pass under an extravagant white stone "canopy" added to the south side by Bishop Louis d'Amboise in the early 16th Century. The single nave, in which the main features are austerity and purity, has a roof of ribbed vaulting and is lit by long narrow stained glass lights that resemble slit windows. The Flamboyant Gothic chancel and roodscreen were added by Louis d'Amboise. Intricate stone carving runs round the entwined motifs, and statues keep watch over the carved wooden choirstalls. Louis d'Amboise also had the gigantic fresco of the Last Judgement painted on the west wall. And last but not least, artists from Bologna decorated the great vaulted roof with numerous portraits of saints.

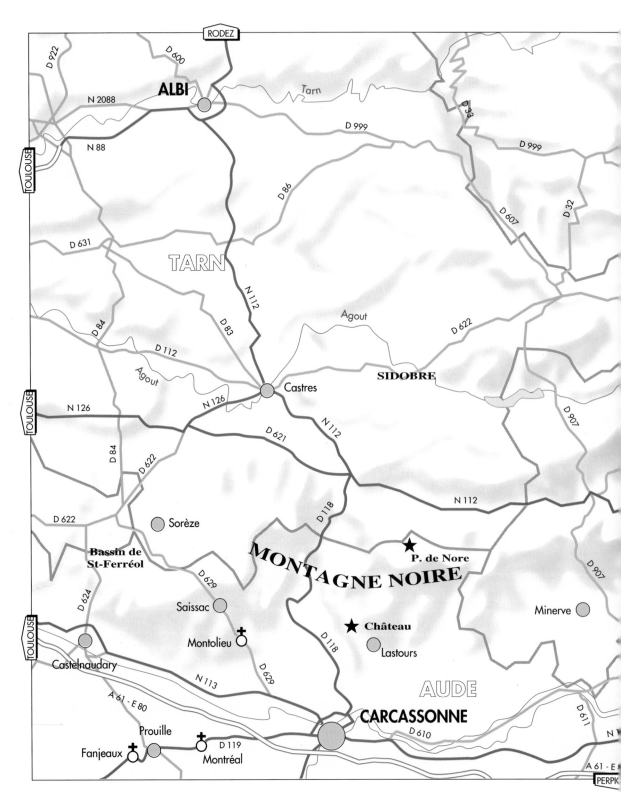

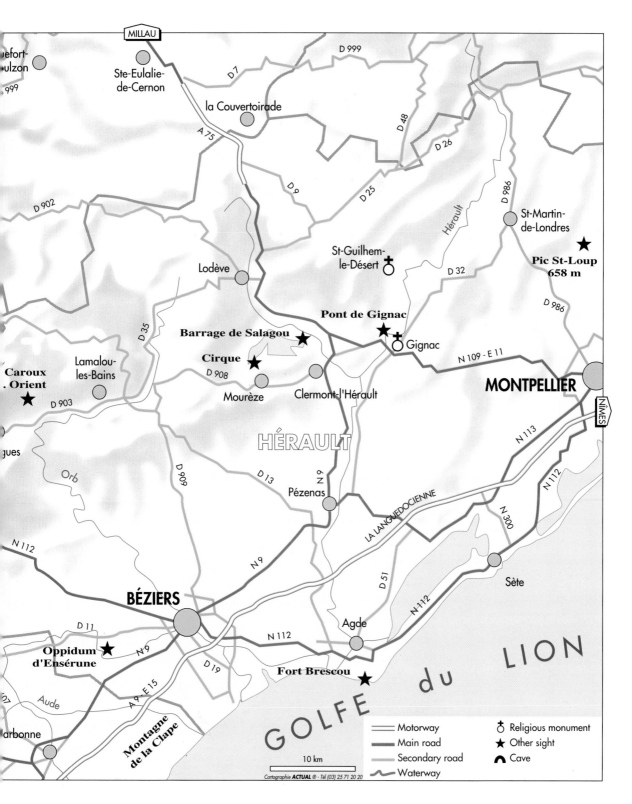

MILLAU

Ste-Eulalie-de-Cernon

quefort-oulzon

D 999

D 999

D 7

la Couvertoirade

D 999

D 48

D 26

A 75

D 9

D 25

Hérault

D 986

St-Martin-de-Londres

St-Guilhem-le-Désert ☿

D 902

Lodève

D 32

Pic St-Loup 658 m ★

D 986

D 35

Pont de Gignac ★ ✝

Barrage de Salagou ★

Gignac ○

Cirque ★

N 109 - E 11

Caroux . Orient ★

Lamalou-les-Bains

D 908

Mourèze

Clermont-l'Hérault

MONTPELLIER

D 903

NÎMES

gues

HÉRAULT

N 113

Orb

D 909

D 13

N 9

Pézenas

N 112

N 112

LA LANGUEDOCIENNE

N 300

N 112

Sète

BÉZIERS

N 9

D 51

N 112

D 11

Agde

Oppidum d'Ensérune ★

N 9

N 112

Fort Brescou ★

D 19

A 9 - E 15

GOLFE du LION

Aude

07

Montagne de la Clape

arbonne

10 km

Cartographie **ACTUAL** ® - Tél (03) 25 71 20 20

Motorway	☿ Religious monument
Main road	★ Other sight
Secondary road	∩ Cave
Waterway	

Wonderful Languedoc-Roussillon

Albi. St. Cecilia's Cathedral, the Old Bridge and La Berbie Palace.

ALBI-STYLE BEEF STEW

Serves 8
Preparation time: 30 minutes
Cooking time: 2 1/2 hours

400 g beef, 800 g shin of veal, 1 ham with bone (500 g), 1 cooked sausage, 1 quarter preserved goose, 2 marrow bones, 1 poultry giblets, 2 carrots, 2 white turnips, 2 leeks (white part only), few sticks of celery, 2 onions, 2 cloves, 1 good-sized cabbage heart, salt, few turns of the pepper mill.

▶ Peel vegetables. Stick cloves in onions. Dice celery, carrots and turnips. Cut white parts of leeks into sections. Tie string round cabbage.

▶ Place beef, veal and ham in large stewpan. Pour in 2 1/2 litres water and bring to boil. Season with salt (remember ham is already salted) and pepper.

▶ Add all vegetables, cover pan, bring back to boil and simmer for 1 1/2 hrs.

▶ Add giblets, sausage, and marrow bones salted at each end. Cook for a further 1 hr.

▶ Carefully remove fat from preserved goose and reheat in stock for 5 mins before end of cooking time.

▶ Serve meat on large platter surrounded by vegetables and stock over slices of stale country loaf.

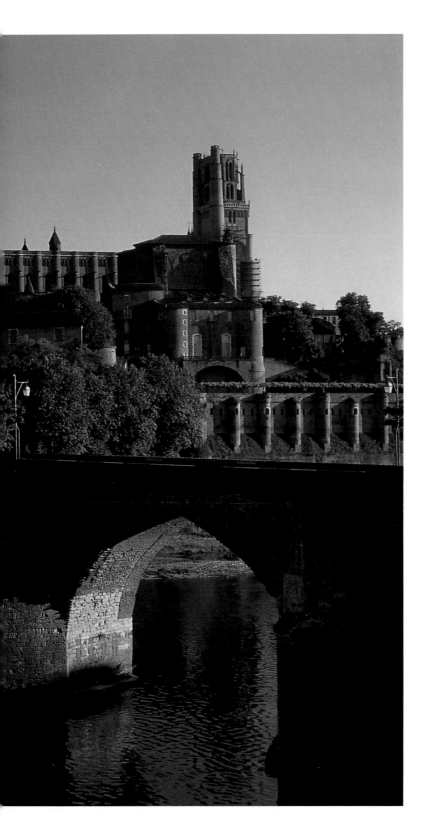

La Berbie Palace, once the Bishop's Palace, was built for Bishop Bernard de Combret c. 1265 A.D. From the 1280's to the end of the Wars of Religion, the palace served as a fortress. Today, it houses the famous Toulouse-Lautrec Museum containing posters, portraits of Valentin le Désossé (the Boneless Man), Aristide Bruant, Jane Avril, and Yvette Guilbert, sketches from the series entitled "The Circus" and the painting called "The Lounge in the Rue des Moulins". All these works show the great talent of this marginal artist who was born and brought up in the neighbourhood.

While in Albi-the-Red-Town, you can also see Toulouse-Lautrec's birthplace, the 16th-century halftimbered Enjalbert Mansion, the 17th-century Reynès Residence with its successive rows of galleries, and St. Salvy's Church, once the collegiate church built partly in the Romanesque period. It still has fine 13th-century cloisters.

A short distance out of town, to the north, is the *Cagnac Mine* in which the gallery in shaft no. 2 has been restored and opened to the public by six former miners. Anybody with a passion for industrial history will also enjoy a visit to *Saint-Juéry,* a spot that is outstanding enough for the Saut-de-Sabo Waterfall. This was the site chosen in the early 19th Century for a metal foundry, with kilns and tilt hammers. In its heyday, the works employed 2,000 people.

A mediaeval pageant.

CATHAR SITES IN AUDE

To the north of the Bugarach peak, in the Corbières region not far from Couiza, lies *Rennes-le-Château,* once a capital of the Visigoths. An atmosphere of mystery has hung over the area since, at the end of last century, its parish priest discovered treasure buried by the Knights Templar. Or so the rumour goes — and it's still repeated today.

The D613 road then leads to the castle at *Arques* founded in 1280 and enlarged in 1316.

Durfort. The castle ruins.

Arques. The 13th-century keep.

Perched high on a rock above the R. Sou, the Cathar fortress of *Termes* withstood a four-month siege led by Simon de Montfort, but the garrison was forced to surrender in November 1210 when water supplies ran out. In the 17th Century, a stonemason from Limoux blew up the outer walls.

The entrance to the Sou Gorge was controlled by Durfort Castle. Its ruins are so steeped in melancholy that the locals describe Durfort as the "Sleeping Beauty's Castle".

To the east, the 13th-century fortress of Villerouge-Termenès stands high above a large mediaeval village. In 1333, Bélibaste, the last Cathar Bishop, was burnt at the stake in the courtyard of the castle.

Above it is a gigantic rectangular keep flanked by towers at all four corners.

From the Orbieu Bridge, the D212 road climbs up the Orbieu Gorge to Auriac Castle. Built in the early 11th Century, it belonged to the lords of *Termes* whose fief lay in Termes itself, a few miles further north.

Auriac. The castle ruins.

Villerouge-Termenès.

Wonderful Languedoc-Roussillon

The formidable walls encircling Carcassonne.

CARCASSONNE

Standing in the shadow of the ramparts at *Carcassonne*, Viollet-le-Duc said, "I do not know that there exists anywhere else in Europe such a complete and formidable defensive structure dating from the 5th, 12th and 13th Centuries." Yet the mediaeval walled town only escaped total destruction by a hair's breadth. In 1850, an

A circular "Cathar" gravestone in the archaeology museum.

official demolition order was signed. Prosper Mérimée, Inspector of Historic Monuments, the architect Viollet-le-Duc and the archaeologist Cros-Mayrevieille succeeded in having the order withdrawn and the military architecture restored. Carcassonne was saved. Today, it is one of the most popular tourist venues in France.

Lying at the narrowest part of the corridor separating the Pyrenees and the Massif Central, on a site ideal for controlling traffic between the Atlantic coast and the Mediterranean or between Spain and France, the hillfort of Carcassonne some 162 ft. above the R.

Aude, was of major strategic importance. It was the site of human habitation in the 11th Century B.C. Then came the Gauls and, finally, the Romans who built a castle and ramparts. These walls can be seen in the north-west section of the inner wall, between the towers called Four-Saint-Nazaire and Moulin-du-Connétable. There are more on the eastern side, between the Davejean and Saint-Sermin Towers and between the Tour du Plô and the Tour des Prisons.

In the 5th Century, the Visigoths strengthened the ramparts. After falling to the Saracen in 725 A.D, the town

The town walls.

resisted siege by the Franks in the 750's. This episode in Carcassonne's history is the subject of a very popular local legend. When the Moorish chieftain died, his widow, Dame Carcas, had straw dummies placed along the battlements, dressed in the armour of dead soldiers. The Franks decided against attack and resolved instead to starve the inhabitants into submission. Soon, all that remained to feed the besieged population was one barrel of food. Dame Carcas gave it all to a sow which she then threw over the walls. The discouraged Franks began negotiations.

The Lords of Trencavel, Viscounts of Carcassonne,

CARCASSONNE-STYLE CAPON

Serves 8
Preparation time : 30 mins **Cooking time**: 1 hr 05 mins.

1 x 2.5 kg capon with neck, 4 chicken livers, 100 g green olives (stoned), 500 g sausagemeat, 1 slice stale country loaf, 1 large onion, 2 cloves garlic, 30 g goose fat, salt, freshly-ground pepper

▶ Peel and chop onion. Peel garlic. Cut bread into small cubes.
▶ Heat goose fat in frying pan over medium heat. Add chicken livers and onions and fry for 5 mins, stirring continuously.
▶ Pour contents of frying pan into bowl and mash roughly with fork. Add sausagemeat and olives. Blend all ingredients. Season with pepper and add salt only if necessary.
▶ Rub bread with cloves of garlic. Place cubes of bread at regular intervals beneath skin of capon neck. Fill capon with stuffing and carefully stitch up openings. Season capon with salt and pepper.
▶ Lay capon on grill of roasting dish. Roast in hot oven (210 °C / Th. 7) for approx. 1 hr.

improved the town. They built the Count's Castle c. 1130; it is a masterpiece of military architecture, a fortress within a fortress. Its towers and curtain walls were topped by hoardings. Viollet-le-Duc had these wooden galleries rebuilt. They were designed to give archers a means of keeping watch on gates and moats. Today, the Count's Castle houses the archaeological museum.

After the Albigensian Crusade, the kings of France annexed Carcassonne (1224-1226). Louis IX and, later, Philip

The "Médiévales" festival.

the Bold consolidated the inner ramparts and commissioned the building of the outer walls over a mile long and bristling with nineteen towers. Lower than the inner ramparts, this wall remained below the line of fire of the defending troops. Any enemy forces who succeeded in passing this first wall found themselves blocked on the jousting grounds, the long passage running between the two walls. A fortified passageway led to the banks of the R. Aude where there was a barbican that has since been replaced by St.

Gimer's Church. The town's four main gates, the Narbonnaise to the east, the Aude to the west, the St. Nazaire to the south and the Rodez on the north side, are wonderful examples of what fortified gateways should be.

Nestling within its ramparts, the whole town has a mediaeval air. The Cathedral of St. Nazaire and St. Celse has an 11th-century Romanesque nave adjacent to a Gothic chancel and transept (1269-1322). The stained glass and statues are outstanding pieces of craftsmanship.

At the foot of the walled town is the Lower Town, a fine example of a checkerboard urban layout. It was built in the reign of St. Louis and it, too, has its treasures — St. Michael's Cathedral that is so typical of Gothic architecture in Languedoc, St. Vincent's Church with its tall 13th-century tower, the 12th-century Old Bridge (*Pont-Vieux*) that separated the two rival districts, the Lower Town and the Walled Town. The Place Carnot and a number of fine private mansions are also worth a look.

Castres. Old houses on the banks of the River Agout.

The former Bishop's Palace.

CASTELNAUDARY

The town famous for its cassoulet is equally well-known for the battle fought on 1st September 1632 in the Fresquel Plain, which opposed Henri de Montmorency, Governor of Languedoc, and the royal army under Richelieu. Montmorency was defeated, arrested and executed in Toulouse. St. Michael's Church has a superb porch-belltower 182 ft. high. On the hill at Le Pech, you can see the Cugarel Mill from which there is a panoramic view of the dazzling Lauragais Plain.

The D103 road leads to *St. Papoul's Abbey*, founded in the 11th Century.

CASTRES

Castres, a wool town and the birthplace of the Socialist politician Jean Jaurès, boasts a Baroque cathedral dedicated to St. Benedict (1677-1718), the Rococo Church of Notre-Dame-de-la-Platé, and most importantly, the Goya Museum in the former Bishop's Palace built in 1699 to designs by Mansard. The museum houses a number of the great Spanish artist's major works e.g. "The Philippine Junta presided over by Ferdinand VII" (1814), the etchings collectively entitled "Caprice" and the "Disasters of War". The palace gardens were laid out by Le Nôtre.

Lauragais Plain.

for female Cathar converts. The convent was destroyed during the French Revolution and replaced by buildings in the Romano-Byzantine style.

Not far from Fanjeaux, on the RN119 road that now bears the name "The St. Dominic Road" is *Montréal* or "Mount Royal", proud site of the colossal St. Vincent's Collegiate Church built in 1317. Inside is a Cavaillé-Coll organ dating from the 18th Century. Legend has it that, when St. Dominic passed through the region, blood seeped out of the corn cut by Cathars in nearby field.

The controversy has lost much of its bitterness but grudges die hard. It was in Fanjeaux that the "Friends of the Cathars" created the famous "Fanjeaux Notebooks" which have published many knowledgeable articles, in particular by René Nelli and Déodat Roché.

FANJEAUX, PROUILLE AND MONTRÉAL, IN THE FOOTSTEPS OF THE PREACHING FRIARS

Fanjeaux. St. Dominic's House, which was turned into a shrine in 1948.

Fanjeaux, Prouille and Montréal are three places held as sacred by the Dominicans. After leaving his native Spain in 1203, Dominic settled in *Fanjeaux* to combat the Cathar heresy. The house where the saint lived from 1206 to 1216 is only 50 yds. from the church. It has undergone major restoration. During a public debate held within the church, the Cathars threw into the fire the manuscript that Dominic was reading. "After being in the flames for some time without smouldering, the document flew out of the fire of its own accord,

which amazed all those present" (Pierre des Vaux de Cernay, *Histoire albigeoise* written in the 13th Century). The miraculous notebook hit one of the rafters in the roof and scorched it. This rafter is piously kept in the church where it hangs from the roof on chains.

On the uplands of the "Segnadou", a memorial stone commemorates another miracle. Dominic was looking at the plains when he saw a ball of fire fall to the ground just over one mile from the town. The comet marked the site of *Prouille* where Dominic was to found a convent

Wonderful Languedoc-Roussillon

LAMALOU-LES-BAINS

*Saint-Pons-de-Thomières.
The minster.*

The sedative waters of *Lamalou* have been used for therapeutic purposes since the Middle Ages. The King of Spain, Sultan of Morocco and Alexandre Dumas the younger all appreciated the qualities of the town. Alphonse Daudet and André Gide were both treated here. Nowadays, people who come here to take the waters can attend operettas as part of the lyric festival staged in the magnificent Italianate theatre. Just over one mile away on the Poujol road is a chapel in the midst of a very modest graveyard. This is *Saint-Pierre-de-Rhèdes* on one of the roads to Compostella. The twin arches in the apse, the strange carved figure in the south wall, and the bas-relief in the nave are all representative of the late Romanesque period (12th Century).

Overlooking Lamalou is *Mont Caroux* (alt. 3,546 ft.), the highest point in the Espinouse range from which there are some splendid views of the Montagne Noire and the Languedoc Plain. On its western slopes, the tiny R. Héric trickles down a cleft in the rock in a series of waterfalls amidst a myriad of muffled sounds.

Saint-Pons-de-Thomières to the west is the centre of the Upper Languedoc Country Park. It boasts a Romanesque minster built in the last quarter of the 12th Century.

Although it then underwent alterations and was restored between 1839 and 1841, the church and erstwhile cathedral is remarkable for its crenelated towers, the "Door of the Deceased" with its enigmatic carvings, the tympani on the West Front, and the upper sections of the former nave, now the sacristy. The Prehistory Museum has a collection of statue-menhirs also known as the "Mute Goddesses".

The RN112 road leads to the *Devèze Cave,* nicknamed the "Glass-spinner's Palace". Discovered in 1886, it was laid out for visitors in 1932. More than 400 yds. of gallery and chamber sparkle with ivory-like rock formations mottled with yellow ochre. There are countless beauty spots and places to visit in the vicinity e.g. the mediaeval village of *La Salvetat-sur-Agout,* the hillfort in *Olonzac,* old houses in *Olargues,* and a bellfoundry in *Hérépian.*

Lamalou-les-Bains.

Lastours.

The ruined castle in Cabaret.

THE FOUR CASTLES
OF LASTOURS

High above the Carcassonne-Mazamet road, keeping watch on the iron convoys travelling from the mines on the Canigou to the foundries at Les Martyrs, and clinging onto a hilltop bristling with cypress trees above the gold-filled Orbiel Valley are the four castles of *Lastours* i.e. Quertinheux, the most southerly of the fortresses, Fleur-Espine the oldest (12th-century), the Régine Tower and the huge Cabaret which got its name from the Latin "caput arietis" or "the ram's head". The five-sided keep in Cabaret contains a chamber with ribbed vaulted roof on the upper storey and a lower chamber with five slit-windows facing the direction of the sunrise during the winter solstice. This, then, is a "solar" castle.

Lastours stands at the end of the "Belvedère" path or, more easily, at the end of a path some 800 yds. from the village on the Ilhes road. Unfortunately, time and the locals who are particularly fond of solid masonry have done much to demolish the walls of Lastours.

A few miles to the east is the Montagne Noire gashed by the vertiginous *Cabrespine Abyss*.

MINERVE, IN THE LAND OF DRUIDS AND CATHARS

A natural bridge in Minerve.

The town walls in Minerve.

Lying astride the Montagne Noire and the Aude Plain, the Minerve region is steeped in memories of the Druids and the Cathars. The main town in the province is a fabulous place, a blend of yellow ochre stones and the bare rock of the Cesse and Briant Gorges. Protected by its ramparts, the town was impregnable. An impressive fortress called the "Castel" closed off the only entrance. Unfortunately, *Minerve* only had one well for its water supply, the Puits Saint-Rustique. Simon de Montfort destroyed it in 1210 and the town was forced to surrender. One hundred and forty Cathars preferred to be burnt at the stake than submit. The remains of the well can still be seen on the scarp slope leading up to the Briant Gorge.

The R. Cesse has gouged out two tunnels at the foot of the town — the "Great Bridge" that measures approx. 357 ft. When the water level is low, in summer, you can walk along them and collect interesting polished stones. Upstream, the Fauzan Cave was used by settlers in prehistoric times. The *La Coquille Cave*, which was discovered in 1927, contains drawings of animals, and traces of human and bear footprints.

Before leaving this region, a visit to *Rieux-Minervois* is a "must". This wine-producing village has an amazing 12th-century Romanesque church. The seven-sided chancel surrounded by an ambulatory in the shape of a rotunda is topped by a dome with a belltower above it. The decorative features show a marked Byzanthine influence.

Minerve.

Mourèze Corrie. Dolomitic rocks.

MOURRÈZE CORRIE

The fountain in Clermont-l'Hérault.

Just a few miles from the vast manmade Salagou lake (750 hectares surrounded by reddish and basalt hills in which fossils several hundred million years old have been discovered near the village of Mérifons) and not far from Clermont-l'Hérault, where the main sights are the old Le Pioch District and the superb Gothic Church of St. Paul in the shadow of a fortress with seven towers, lies the Mourèze corrie, an extraordinary jumble of magnesian limestone rocks worn away into strange shapes. In an amphitheatre covering an area of 340 hectares, rugged rocks jut up out of copses, looking like the ruins of some erstwhile citadel. Depending on your imagination, you might see them as monsters' heads, chimera, demons or fairies.

Erosion has carved out some impressive shapes.

SAINT-GUILHEM-LE-DÉSERT, FOR A SOVEREIGN TURNED MONK

Saint-Guilhem-le-Désert.
A gallery in the abbey cloisters.

The chevet of the church.

*S*aint-Guilhem used to be called Gellone. The monastery took the name of Guillaume of Aquitaine, Count of Toulouse, better-known as Guillaume Fierabras, or "William the Short-Nosed". This grandson of Charles Martel and trusted advisor to Charlemagne had spent his life waging war on the Saracen. Then he retired to the abbey that he founded in Gellone. From 806 A.D. to his death in 812 A.D. he led the life of a simple monk.

You cannot fully appreciate the majestic harmony of Saint-Guilhem-le-Désert unless you climb the goat tracks clinging onto the rock face high above the village. From there, the church, cloisters and monastery buildings seem to be suspended in mid air above the Verdus Ravine. The minster, which has a magnificent Romanesque chevet, used to house the relic of the True Cross given by Charlemagne to his friend Guillaume.

The original church no longer exists; the present building was consecrated in 1076 A.D. The narthex and nave date from this period. The apse and transept were added in the late 11th Century. The tower-porch was built in the 12th-15th Centuries. In the church, note the dark semi-circular barrel vaulting, the disproportionate contrast between the narrow nave and the wide apse, and the wonderful semi-circular Romanesque vaulting in the apse. Digs carried out in 1962-65 revealed a crypt that is now open to the public. It was part of the Pre-Romanesque 10th-

The rooftops of Saint-Guilhem.

In the narrow streets of Saint-Guilhem.

century church and once housed St. William's tomb.

On the south side, the church used to be bordered by admirable two-storey cloisters. They were used by a local stonemason as a ready supply of raw material. The Americans found some fragments, which they have reconstructed as part of the Cloisters in New-York. Only the north and west galleries remain in Saint-Guilhem, and parts of them have been reconstructed. The refectory and its ribbed vaulting to the west of the cloisters has been saved from destruction. Some sections of the upper cloisters, carved fragments and precious works of art have been brought together in an archaeological museum. A 12th-century white marble altar incrusted with pieces of coloured glass, St. Guilhem's tomb, and an ancient stone coffin dating from the 6th-7th Centuries, said to have contained the mortal remains of St. William's sisters, are the monastery's most outstanding exhibits.

Before you leave Saint-Guilhem, stop at the Devil's Bridge *(Pont du Diable)* built across the R. Hérault in the 10th Century at a place known as the "Black Abyss" *(Gouffre Noir)*. Not far from the bridge, the *Clamouse cave* (the so-called "Screamer") contains some impressive resurgences and chambers filled with fabulous rock formations sparkling with ice crystals. In *Gignac*, the three-arched bridge over the R. Hérault is one of the finest 18th-century bridges in France.

Saint-Martin-de-Londres.

SAINT-MARTIN-DE-LONDRES

"Londres" comes from the Occitan word "loudro" meaning "marshland". Isolated by scrub in a basin that was once a swamp but later drained, *Saint-Martin-de-Londres* surprises visitors for the unsophisticated charm of its mediaeval streets and old houses huddling round the church. Building work began on the sanctuary itself, which depends on Saint-Guilhem, in the late 11th Century. Almost the entire building is in the Early Romanesque style.

Just over six miles to the east of the village is the *Pic Saint-Loup* whose long sheer-sided ridge juts up above the scrub (alt. 2,138 ft). From the top, there is a panoramic view across the Cévennes, the Alpilles, the Camargue and the Mediterranean coastline.

Cambous on the south-facing slope, has a strange set of huts, reconstructions of buildings from the Copper Age.

People with an interest in industrial heritage will enjoy a visit to *Ferrières-les-Verreries* near Saint-Bauzille-de-Putois, the Couloubrines glassworks dating from the Renaissance and the art glassworks in *Claret*.

SAISSAC AND THE MONTAGNE NOIRE

In the high season, the village of *Saissac* perched above the Vernassonne Ravine sparkles with a fabulous son et lumière that brings back to life the "Courts of Love" of days gone by. Bertrand de Saissac's feudal fortress stands at the tip of a spur of rock. Two massive keeps, one of them four-sided and the other polygonal, constitute the defensive heart of the building.

South on the D629 road is *Montolieu,* a booklovers' dream. Thanks to an association called *La Mémoire du Livre,* fourteen bookshops, copyists, and a

The Saint-Ferréol Basin. The dike.

The Saint-Ferréol Basin.
The water spout.

bookbinder have turned this village into a minor literary capital.

From Saissac or Revel, there are numerous routes crisscrossing the *Montagne Noire* whether you are travelling by car or on foot. There is a 19-mile footpath running along the banks of the ditch designed by Riquet as a catch drain for the Canal du Midi. From the catchment basin in Alzeau to the huge reservoir at *Saint-Ferréol,* the delightful path wends its way past stream and waterfall through the woodland.

Sorèze is worth a visit for its 13th-century octagonal bell-tower, all that remains of the abbey founded in the 9th Century by Pippin of Aquitaine. The school in Sorèze is famous because it was one of the first establishments to offer teaching in geography, history, mathematics and foreign languages. The most famous name connected with the college is Lacordaire who died there in 1861 and is buried in the chapel.

Last but not least, how about a climb to the summit of the *Pic de Nore* (alt. 3,935 ft), the highest peak in the Montagne Noire range. From it, the view extends as far as the Canigou.

LE SIDOBRE, BOULDERS STEEPED IN MYSTERY

Peyro-Clabado. 780 tonnes of precariously-balanced rock.

The granite faults undermined by erosion form a fantastic landscape of rocks on the *Sidobre Plateau.* Like enormous balls balancing precariously on top of each other, the rocks have unbelievable shapes. They are known as the Priest's Hat, Three Cheeses, Goose Rock, Napoleon's Hat etc. These are easy, sometimes annoying, comparisons. Yet it is impossible not to be impressed by the gigantic rocks that seem about to tumble down and crush onlookers at any moment. A mere length of timber is sufficient to lever and shake the Seven Scythe Rock (Roc des Sept-Faux) which weighs 900 metric tonnes. And nobody really dares to touch the Peyro-Clabado block of granite for its 780 tonnes are supported by nothing more than a narrow ridge.

The footpaths through the woods and across the moors take ramblers past some magnificent sights — caves, ponds and lakes, rivers of rock called "compayrés" and the Trout Ladder (Saut de Truite) where the R. Lignon flows into a waterfall some 65 ft. high. And often a slight trickle indicates the presence of a stream hidden beneath the rocks.

A river of rocks.

Caves and gorges in the Causses and Cévennes

MONT AIGOUAL
AND THE BRAMABIAU ABYSS

Pastures on the slopes of Mont Aigoual.

The name *Aigoual* comes from the Latin "Aiqualis" meaning "damp", for the highest peak in the *Cévennes*, standing at 5,093 ft, is one of the water towers for the Massif Central. Rainfall is high and this has resulted in a veritable hydrographic network with the rivers Hérault, Jonte and Dourbie, the last two being tributaries of the R. Tarn. On the top of the mountain is a met. station from which there is an exceptionally wide panoramic view of the Mediterranean coast, the Pyrenees, and the Alps. The slopes are covered with forests, a paradise for walkers.

To the west, where the Cévennes meet the Causses, there are two places of interest that are worth going out of your way to visit. Near Villemagne are the abandoned remains of the silver lead mines. Near Camprieu, the *Bramabiau Abyss* is the extraordinary resurgence of the tiny stream called Bonheur, transformed here into a waterfall. "Bramabiau" means "lowing of oxen". When the stream is in spate, the roar is impressive. Since Edouard-Alfred Martel's initial exploration in 1888, six miles of galleries have been discovered. Nowadays, it is possible to pass through the dark crevice from which the waterfall flows and on into an underground universe that is a fascinating succession of long cracks and narrow corridors.

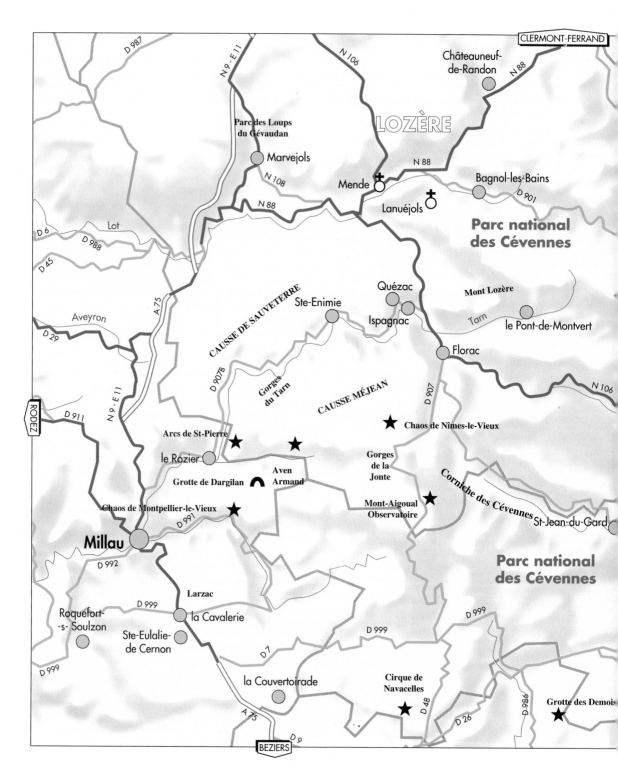

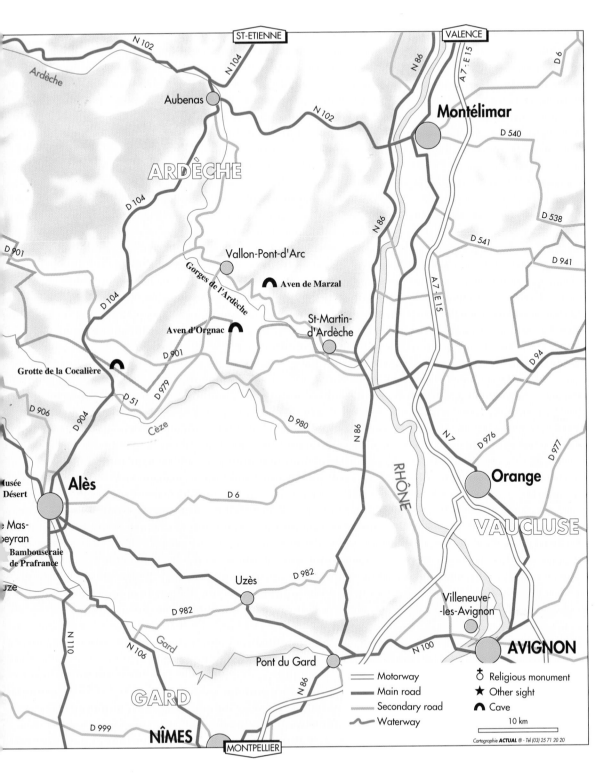

ST-ETIENNE

N 102

VALENCE

N 104

Ardèche

N 86

A 7 - E 15

D 6

Aubenas

N 102

Montélimar

D 540

ARDÈCHE

D 104

N 86

D 538

D 901

Vallon-Pont-d'Arc

Gorges de l'Ardèche

Aven de Marzal

D 541

D 941

D 104

Aven d'Orgnac

St-Martin-d'Ardèche

A 7 - E 15

D 901

D 94

Grotte de la Cocalière

D 51

D 979

D 906

D 904

Cèze

D 980

N 86

RHÔNE

N 7

D 976

D 977

Alès

D 6

N 86

Orange

VAUCLUSE

usée
Désert

e Mas-
peyran

**Bambouseraie
de Prafrance**

uze

D 982

Uzès

Villeneuve-
les-Avignon

D 982

Gard

N 110

N 106

Pont du Gard

N 86

N 100

AVIGNON

GARD

Motorway

Main road

Secondary road

Waterway

⚲ Religious monument

★ Other sight

◠ Cave

10 km

D 999

NÎMES

MONTPELLIER

Cartographie ACTUAL ® - Tél (03) 25 71 20 20

THE ARDÈCHE GORGE

Why not start your visit at the Arc Bridge *(Pont de l'Arc)*, a monumental arch of rock 111 ft. high and 192 ft. wide? The *Ardèche Gorge* narrows further on in a series of carefree meanders and roaring rapids. Each of the many observation platforms is worth a stop — Serre de Tourre, Gaud, Autridge, Gournier, La Madeleine (a platform above the ramparts of the Upper Cliff Road destined to take your breath away).

On the north side of this cliff is the *Madeleine Cave* with its galleries, tunnels, and chambers covered with rock formations. Four miles further north on the Plateau des Gras, hidden for many years beneath evergreen oak thickets, is the *Marzal Aven* which devoured imprudent men or animals. An almost vertical flight of steps cut into the sides of the swallow-hole leads down to the Tomb Chamber where numerous bones were discovered. The visit continues with the Dog Chamber and ends with the Diamond Chamber 423 ft. below the ground.

Back in the Gorge, you can admire the views from the Cathédrale, Balcon des Templiers, Grand Belvedère, Colombier and Ranc Pointu. In Saint-Martin-d'Ardèche, take the CD 174 road to the famous swallow-hole at *Orgnac*. Robert de Joly first explored it in 1935 but potholers are still finding new galleries in this incredible network of underground passages. The dark red colour of some of the old lava flows, the size of the rock formations, and the mystery of the unexplored corridors are sure to fascinate visitors to the swallow-hole that is generally considered to be one of the most beautiful anywhere in the world.

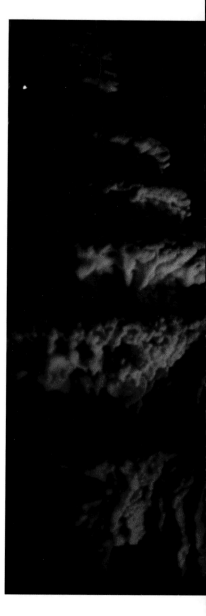

AVEN ARMAND

One September's day in 1897, *Louis Armand*, a locksmith in the village of Rozier, discovered an incredible abyss in the heart of the Causse Méjean. He immediately contacted his friend, the pot-holer Edouard-Alfred Martel, who was always in search of new swallow-holes.

Exploration started on 19th September. At the bottom of the abyss, some 224 ft. below ground level, Louis Armand found "a dream out of the Arabian Nights": "Stupendous! Magnificent! More beautiful than Dargilan! A veritable forest of stone!"

Since 1926, this subterranean wonder of the world has been open to the public. A tunnel 611 ft. long was dug out to give direct access to the foot of the well, in a chamber measuring 163 ft. by 326 ft. and 114 ft. high, where 400 fanstastically-shaped stalagmites rise to

Caves and gorges in the Causses and Cévennes

L'Aven Armand. The "Tropical Jungle".

heights of over 80 ft. It is an "untouched forest" of a thousand arabesques sparkling with naturally-cut crystal. On the other side, an opaque shadow indicates an abyss that is even deeper than this one but closed by a rockfall 637 ft. below ground level.

The Causse Méjean includes two other spectacular sights - the rocks of *Nimes-le-Vieux* to the east where gigantic blocks of limestone are shaped like ruined buildings, and the Arcs de Saint-Pierre to the west, a rocky corrie where numerous prehistoric remains have been found.

Take advantage of these excursions to go and stroke the amazing Przewalski horses bred in *Hures-la-Parade* and to visit the typical Causses farm in *Hyelsas*.

Wonderful Languedoc-Roussillon

The Cévennes cliff road.

THE CÉVENNES
CLIFF ROAD

From Florac to Saint-Jean-du-Gard, the CD 9 road which has been given the name *"Corniche des Cévennes"* runs through the National Park high above the Française du Gardon de Sainte-Croix Valley to the north-east and the Borgne du Gardon de Saint-Jean Valley to the south-west. This was the country of the "Camisards", Protestant rebels "in shirt sleeves" who refused to submit to the dragoons sent in by Louis XIV. Sometimes, they would meet in *La Can de l'Hospitalet* among the strange rocks that look like the ruins of temple. Beyond *l'Hospitalet,* a place of refuge for lost travellers, the limestone plateau provides a splendid view of Mount Lozère and Mount Aigoual whose slopes are smothered in trees. In Saint-Flour-de-Pompidou, the limestone gives way to schist. The hilltop road twists and turns from one rise to the other, giving wonderful panoramic views until it runs in a series of bends down to Saint-Jean-du-Gard.

Caves and gorges in the Causses and Cévennes

THE LAND OF THE KNIGHTS TEMPLAR

Once the property of the Knights Templar and, later, of the Knights of St. John of Jerusalem, *La Couvertoirade* is a remarkable fortified village which still has its 15th-century walls, parts of its 12th-14th century castle, a fortress-church and houses from the Renaissance period.

All around it, the arid *Larzac* has a thousand secrets to reveal to those in search of adventure - unexpected swallow-holes, yaw-

La Couvertoirade. A fortified gateway.

Rocks on the Larzac Plateau.

Sainte-Eulalie-de-Cernon, a Knights Templar commandery.

ning abysses, phantom-like rocks, cliffs and gorges, dry river beds, tumbling underground rivers rushing out into the daylight, villages with houses roofed with stone slabs, old feudal towers, and fortified gateways (see *La Cavalerie, Sainte-Eulalie-de-Cornon,* a superb fortress and a former commandery of the Knights Templar), chapels lost in the wilderness (e.g. in *La Salvage*), shepherds' huts, farms that blend right into the surrounding rocks. And everywhere the same landscape — like a scene straight out of a cowboy film.

Ewes on a farm in Sainte-Eulalie (Cantal).

Wonderful Languedoc-Roussillon

·THE DEMOISELLES CAVE

The swallow-hole on the Thaurac Plateau used to terrify local peasants. They thought it was the entrance to the land of the Little People, or "Demoiselles". The *Grotte des Demoiselles* provided refuge for the Protestant rebels during Louis XIV's reign and for nonjuring priests during the French Revolution. It was explored by Edouard-Alfred Martel in 1884, 1889 and 1897. An indefinable atmosphere of ill-being seeps from the stalactite-filled chambers and corridors, some of them very narrow, their walls covered with rock formations. Suddenly, a gallery opens onto a gigantic nave 390 ft. long, 260 ft. wide and 163 ft. high. This "cathedral" of silence, suffused in an evanescent mist, models the translucent rocks into disturbing shapes — the "organ loft", the "Madonna and Child" etc.

THE JONTE GORGE AND DARGILAN CAVE

Over a distance of more than 13 miles from Meyrueis to Le Rozier, the R. Jonte carves out a gorge between the Causse Méjean to the north and the Causse Noir on the left bank. The foaming torrent born on the northern slopes of the Aigoual seems to tremble beneath the hanging outcrops of dolomite

La Jonte Gorge.

rocks on the Causse Noire, while the limestone of the Méjean with its crevice-filled bastions imitates the sumptuous fantasies of palaces from the Arabian Nights.

The cliffs are riddled with caves such as La Vigne and La Chèvre on the north slope where human and bear bones have been discovered, dating from the Quaternary Era. Dug into the cliff face of the Causse Noir is the famous *Dargilan Cave,* which was discovered by accident. In 1880, a shepherd named Sahuquet saw a fox run into a bush beneath some rocks. The shepherd struggled to follow it and found himself looking into what he thought was the entrance to hell. He ran away but his adventure intrigued pot-holers. In 1888, Edouard-Alfred Martel began to explore the cave. The Great Chamber is 1,500 yds. long and 113 ft. high. At the end of it are the Rose Chamber and the Mosque, mirages of iridescent stalagmites. A natural well then leads to the petrified Waterfalls, the Lake, the Labyrinth, the Bear Chamber and, finally, to the famous tower that is 65 ft. high.

A typical Lozère farmhouse and Mount Lozère.

LANGOGNE AND CHÂTEAUNEUF-DE-RANDON, IN THE FOOT-STEPS OF DU GUESCLIN

*L*angogne is a town steeped in history with mediaeval, Renaissance and Classical buildings. Its houses are huddled round the Church of St. Gervais and St. Protais that once attracted pilgrims who came here to pray to Our Lady the All-Powerful. A Gothic bridge and 18th-century corn market add to the impression of otherworldliness. Le Calquières threadmill is a four-storey building that is a unique example of an old-fashioned production plant.

From Langogne, you can visit the manmade *Naussac Lake* which swallowed up an entire village. There is also the feudal castle of *Le Luc* (12th Century) standing guard over the borders of the Gévaudan and Vivarais areas; it is interesting for its "ear-of-corn" architecture. Further south, in the town of Bastide-Puylaurent, the Thord Dolmen serves as a remin-

der of the Druids. The Mercoire Forest leads to *Châteauneuf-de-Randon* where a museum and a famous statue commemorate Bertrand Du Guesclin who died here on 14th July 1380 while laying siege to the town.

MOUNT LOZÈRE

*M*ount Lozère to the north of the Cévennes National Park has an altitude of 5,424 ft. Although it is gradually being deserted, the mountain has much to show interested visitors. High above the Chassezac Gorge, for example, is the castle of *La Garde-Guérin*. Its 12th-cen-

The standing stone in La Vayssière.

Mount Lozère.

tury keep 68 ft. high towers over a group of 27 fortified houses that were once occupied by the 27 lords responsible for protecting merchants travelling along the Régordane Way between Auvergne and Languedoc. The castle chapel, which has become the parish church, is a gem of Romanesque architecture.

To the east, the Villefort Dam has drowned the Alter Gorge, creating a vast lake. A dike saved the beautiful castle of Castanet from the waters. It is a 15th-16th century manor house with truncated corner turrets comprising a number of guns.

Le Pont-de-Montvert on the southern slopes of Mont Lozère is filled with memories of the murder of Abbot du Chayla by 53 Protestant conspirators. It was 24th July 1702 and the Protestant rebellion was about to start.

Finally, to the west beyond *Runes* and its waterfall, *La*

Montvert Bridge.

Vayssière has a field full of standing stones that prehistorians find particularly fascinating. *Lanuéjols* to the north has a Roman mausoleum and *Saint-Julie-du-Tournel* boasts a superb fortress. The spa town of *Bagnols-les-Bains* grew up around a spring that is rich in bicarbonate of sulphur, fluoride and rare metals. The water gushes out at a temperature of 41.5 °C.

THE WOLVES OF LE GÉVAUDAN

Marvejols is famous for its fortified gates - Soubeyran, Le Théron and Chanelles, all of which serve as reminders of the struggle by troops led firstly by Du Guesclin and, later, by Admiral de Joyeuse during the Wars of Religion. North of Marvejols, between the Crueize and "l'Enfer" Valleys, and near the village of *Sainte-Lucie,* more than one hundred wolves live in semi-liberty, all of them the debonair descendants of the Beast of Le Gévaudan.

If you drive through the Lot Valley, take time to stop in *Chanac* where the Domaine des Champs has been skilfully turned into a mediaeval time warp with farmstead, workshops, tavern and banqueting hall.

LE MAS-SOUBEYRAN, A CENTRE OF PROTESTANT RESISTANCE

This is a holy place for members of the Reformed Religion. After being marginalised by the Revocation of the Edict of Nantes (1685), persecuted by the dragoons sent in by Louis XIV (their actions were known as "dragonnades") and pursued after the Camisard ("Shirt-Sleeve") Revolt of 1702, the Protestants abandoned their hopeless guerilla actions after the death of their leader, Roland, who was killed in 1704.

The *Mas-Soubeyran,* once Roland's house, is now a "Museum of the Wilderness". The bedroom, the hiding-place where he took shelter when danger loomed, and the kitchen are all still as they used to be. In one room, there is a collection of more than eighty Bibles, many of them priceless exhibits, gifts from Huguenot families. A large collection of documents traces the history of the Protestant resistance in the "wilderness" of the Cévennes until the Edict of Tolerance published in 1787.

Mende. Notre-Dame Bridge and the River Lot.

Mende and its cathedral seen from St. Privat's Hermitage.

Mende. Houses on the banks of the River Lot.

An adjacent building comme-morates the martyrs of this revolt. The visit ends in the reconstruc-ted interior of a typical Cévennes house.

Each year, on the first Sunday in September, nearly twenty thousand Protestants come toge-ther at the Mas.

Nearby is the huge *Trabuc Cave*, the "cave of the one hun-dred thousand soldiers" which provided a place of refuge for the Camisard rebels, and later for bri-gands known as the Trabucaires.

MENDE, THE "UNRIVALLED"

*M*ende, the gateway to the Causses, was the capital of the Gévaudan region before beco-ming the county town of Lozère. Built on the left bank of the R. Lot, the town grew up around the tomb of St. Privat who was

martyred in Mende c. 265 A.D. and buried on the spot where the cathedral stands today. The impressive Gothic sanctuary dominates the entire town. It was built in the early years of the One Hundred Years' War (1368) on the instructions of Pope Urban V who was born in the Gévaudan area. But the great 273-foot tower dates only from 1508; the smaller tower was built the following year. In 1579, Captain Merle and his Hugenots captured Mende. They blew up the cathedral except for the towers, and smashed the "Nonsuch", the largest bell in the Christian world. The buildings were reconstructed between 1599 and 1605. The chancel contains magnificent carved wooden stalls. The crypt, which is one of the oldest in France, contains St. Privat's tomb.

In the old, narrow streets you may come across the 17th-century Town Hall, the Ignon-Fabre Museum housing a number of collections dating from Prehistoric times, the Penitents' Tower (the remains of the 12th-century fortifications), the Consul's House, the former Carmelite Convent (14th Century), the former synagogue (12th Century) and the 13th-century Notre-Dame Bridge across the R. Lot. Like the locals who are so fond of their home, you could then do no better than to walk up to Mont Mimat and go on a pilgrimage to St. Privat's hermitage.

BEAUTIFUL MILLAU

In the first century A.D., *Millau* was famous for its de luxe pottery produced in the workshops in La Graufesenque to the south of the town and distributed throughout the Roman Empire from Pompei to Scotland. A number of remarkable vases, most of them almost intact, have survived to the present day. They are displayed in the town's museum and in the Fenaille Museum in Rodez. This activity was gradually replaced by tanning and, since the Middle Ages, Millau has been the capital of the kid glove industry.

Millau. Place du Maréchal-Foch.

Caves and gorges in the Causses and Cévennes

Millau. Skins for sale.

Rocks in Montpellier-le-Vieux.

In the old town huddling within a meander of the R. Tarn, you can enjoy a stroll beneath the mediaeval arcades on the Place du Maréchal-Foch and along the picturesque alleyways lined with old townhouses. The main places of interest are Notre-Dame Church, a Romanesque building that underwent alteration in the 17th Century, the square belltower (12th Century) topped by an octagonal tower in the 17th Century, a 15th-century mill that juts out into the waters of the Tarn, and a pretty 18th-century wash-house.

On the left bank of the R. Tarn is the *Dourbie Canyon*. From Millau to l'Espérou, the river cuts deep into the Causse forming gorges that are almost 1,000 ft. deep in places. Some of the villages, e.g. *Cantobre,* blend almost completely into the gigantic walls of rugged rock behind them.

MONTPELLIER-LE-VIEUX, WHERE NATURE BECOMES SUPERNATURAL

Montpellier-le-Vieux is a gigantic masterpiece. The jumble of rocks forming this petrified "town" created by erosion cling onto the steep slopes of the Causse Noir 1,300 ft. above the R. Dourbie. Pillars, huge arches, corridors, tiers of seats, colossal piles of rocks, and natural fortresses all have a name — the Mycene Gate, Cyrano's Nose, Harlequin's Head, the Camel, the Sphynx etc. The Obscure Comfort Cave was once a bear's den and the whole area was believed to be

the haunt of Satan. Local people never mentioned this isolated place hidden behind its natural ramparts. It was not until 1883 that local journalists first wrote about Montpellier-le-Vieux. The Douminal rocks, the Ramparts (2,698 ft.) and the Observation Platform provide some wonderful views of this stillborn capital of the Causses.

NAVACELLES CORRIE

*N*avacelles is much-appreciated by geographers who consider it to be an excellent example of a former meander. The R. Vis used to curve its way through an impressively steepsided gorge but the pressure of the water finally cut through the rocky peak that had forced it into the meander, and the meander itself dried up.

Navacelles always delights visitors who are seeing it for the first time. The sheer size of the semicircular corrie, the strange hillfort shaped like a vanilla slice of rocks standing all alone in the centre, the former river bed with its luxurious vegetation, the few houses clinging onto the ridges, the overall harmony of the colours and the delicious impression of freshness in the midst of the arid Causses, make Navacelles an unforgettable place.

From Navacelles, you can take a trip to *Ganges,* which tra-

Rocks in Montpellier-le-Vieux.

ded in precious metals in the days of the Ancient Romans and silk in the days of the Renaissance. Until nylon stockings came onto the market, Ganges used to produce 80,000 pairs of silk stockings every year. Downstream from Ganges is the fortified village of *Laroque* where there is a fine 19th-century threadmill.

ROQUEFORT

Built in tiers up the rugged side of the limestone Cambalou Ridge, Roquefort-sur-Soulzon is world-famous for its ewe's milk cheese. The animals graze on the nearby Larzac Plateau and Causses. Roquefort cheese, which was considered a delicacy in Roman times, owes its particular taste to the quality of the milk, the addition to the curds of the "penicillium roqueforti", a mould found growing in local caves, and the ripening techniques used. The cheese is matured in the caves that riddle the Cambalou. They are damp, at a constant temperature of between 5 and 7°C., and kept continually ventilated by the draughts that circulate between the natural chimneys called "fleurines". The penicillium develops and forms the bluish-green veins that are the trade mark of Roquefort cheese. It takes three months to ripen and is then ready to be sold throughout Europe and in America.

Navacelles Corrie.

Saint-Enimie. A procession to the Hermitage Cave.

MARGERIDE AND AUBRAC, ON THE BORDERS OF CANTAL

Saint-Chély-d'Apcher is an ideal starting point for walks in the granite uplands of La Margeride which rise to an altitude of 5,041 ft. at the Signal de Randon, or on the Aubrac Plateau where the stone walls and peat bogs are strangely reminiscent of the Scottish moors. Almost deserted roads take you into the heart of wide open spaces that have been forgotten by man where you will find some marvellous villages and some unhoped-for beauty spots e.g. *Le Malzieu* and its clock tower on the banks of the R. Truyère, *Sainte-Eulalie* which boasts a 170-hectare park grazed by bison, *Saint-Alban-sur-Limagnole* and its superb church, *Fournels*, *Nasbinals* and the shepherds' huts in Canuc, or *La Baume*, a country house with all the luxury of the 18th Century, something of a surprise in an area that seems to have come from another world.

Florac.

THE TARN GORGE

Over a distance of 56 miles between Florac and Le Rozier, the *Tarn Gorge* gouges out a course between the *Causse du Sauveterre* to the north and the Causse *Méjean* along faults with gigantic walls of rock. This is a paradise for those who enjoy rambling, climbing, potholing or canoeing.

Florac, "Flower of the Waters", is reflected in the Tarnon at the foot of the Causse Méjean. Its tranquil river banks give little indication of the rushing water in the nearby canyon. Beyond the still-quiet village of Ispignac whose Romanesque church and Renaissance houses seem to be sleeping amidst the surrounding orchards, on the other side of the bridge (rebuilt in the 17th Century) and beyond the famous pilgrim's church in *Quézac*, the Tarn begins to flow through a narrower passageway. The castles of Rocheblave and Charbonnières, and the mediaeval fortress of *Castelbouc* high up on a spur of rock some 195 ft. above the river, keep watch and herald the arrival of *Sainte-Enimie*, the main town in the gorge, nestling between sheer cliffs 1,950 ft. high and less than one-and-a-half miles apart.

The wonderful scenery in the canyon called for a legend. Enimie was a Merovingian princess afflicted with leprosy. One evening, an angel told her that the spring at Burle in the Gévaudan area could cure her illness. After a long trip, Enimie reached the banks of the Tarn and a shepherd pointed to the spring. The princess' skin became "as white as pure milk". The girl ordered a monastery to be built near the spring but every Saturday the Devil emerged from a neighbouring swallow-hole and destroyed the previous week's work. Enimie caught him in the act and pursued him through the gorge as far as the Pas du Souci. Night fell. The girl called on the mysterious powers of the mountain to help her. Enormous rocks tumbled down onto the Devil who only just had time to squeeze through a crack and return to Hell.

Believers still come to pray in Sainte-Enimie, at the Burle Spring, in the monastery, and in the cave where Enimie ended her days as a recluse. The rock she used as a bed is still visible

Cobbled streets in Saint-Enimie.

A traditional house in Ispagnac.

today. Water oozing from the rock is said to cure skin disorders.

Scattered from one end of the gorge to the other are the gigantic rocks that were moved by the saint. The *Saint-Chély Corrie*, which looks like the end of the world, is riddled with caves. The Pougnadoires Corrie is

Quézac. The bridge over the River Tarn.

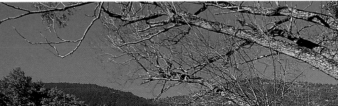

Baumes Corrie.

Caves and gorges in the Causses and Cévennes

Le Rozier with the roads leading to the plateaux of Causse Noir and Causse Méjean.

The village of Les Vignes.   *Castelbouc and its fort.*

filled with cave dwellings. After a brief pause to consider the romantic Château de la Caze (15th Century), the gorge narrows to form the Straits (*"Détroits"*), widens momentarily into the Baumes Corries, and disappears beneath the awesome pile of rocks in the Pas du Souci where the Tarn flows under the stones. The enormous Roque-Sourde that was hurled at Satan lies at the bottom. The Roche-Aiguille was halted midway but remains at an angle. From the top of the cliffroad 1,398 ft. above the river, at the Point-Sublime, there is a panoramic view of scenery that seems to have escaped from the pages of Dante, stretching from the Straits to the Pas du Souci.

At the confluence of the rivers Tarn and Jonte, the peaceful village of Le Rozier marks the end of the gorge beneath the impressive gaze of vultures. A local architecture museum describes life in Lozère in bygone days.

Saint-Enimie and the River Tarn.

From Cévennes to Camargue

AIGUES-MORTES, TWO DEPARTURES FOR THE CRUSADES

Aigues-Mortes. The town walls.

The walls of *Aigues-Mortes*, literally "stagnant waters", emerge from the surrounding marshes and lagoons, bristling with twenty round or square towers of sun-scorched stone. A sight that has something oriental about it. Even the history of this ghostly walled town resembles a legend. Louis IX, who was preparing to set off on a Crusade in the Holy Land, needed a harbour on the Mediterranean Coast. Narbonne had silted up; Marseilles was not French. In 1237, the sovereign came to an arrangement with the lordly abbots of the Psalmodi Monastery and purchased this village not far from the sea. He ordered the construction of a formidable keep, the *Constance Tower*, and the digging of a harbour and canal onto the Mediterranean. On 28th July 1248, fifty thousand men embarked for the Seventh Crusade which was to take them to Egypt. In 1270, Louis set off again from Aigues-Mortes; it was to be his last expedition.

It was St. Louis' son Philip the Bold who completed the work on the rectangular bastion measuring 540 yds. by 325 yds. and the wall with its nine gates, designed by an engineer from

Wonderful Languedoc-Roussillon

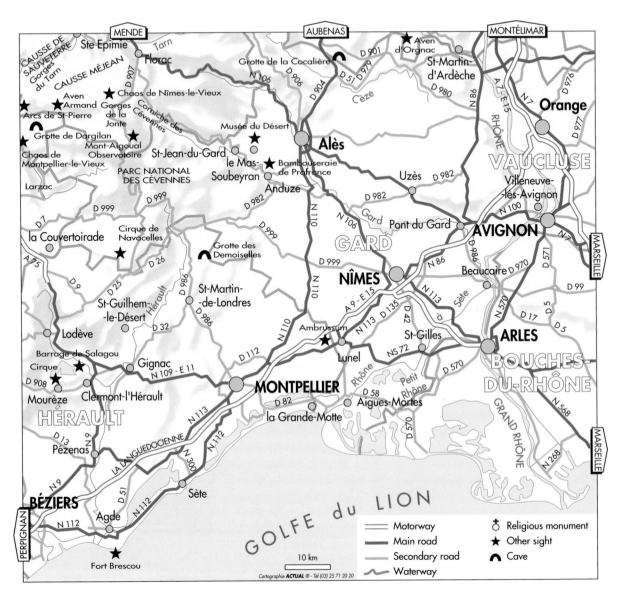

Genoa named Boccanegra. For a century, the harbour was extremely busy, then the channels began to silt up. The One Hundred Years' War caused enormous damage. In 1418, the Armagnac faction massacred Burgundian soldiers, covered their bodies with salt, and threw them into the tower that was thereafter known as the *"Burgundians' Tower"*. During the Wars of Religion, the Constance Tower was turned into a prison and used for Protestant captives. When the harbour was laid out in Sète in 1666, it sounded the final death-knell for Aigues-Mortes. Since then, the town has stood as motionless as a mediaeval mirage.

Aigues-Mortes.

Alès seen from the Hermitage.

ALÈS

*A*lès is famous for the peace treaty signed there by Louis XIII and the Protestants in 1629. The town, which specialises in the breeding of silkworms and the manufacture of silk, still remembers Louis Pasteur who came to rid it of the pebrine epidemic that was killing off the worms. The scientist's stay here was marked by a series of domestic crises — he lost his father and two of his daughters at that time. Alès, though, is also a major industrial town receiving raw materials from coal, iron ore and lead mines. A total of 704 yds. of galleries in one of the mines gives a precise insight into the history of mining.

ANDUZE, THE GENEVA
OF THE CÉVENNES

Nestling close to the slopes of Mount Saint-Julien and protected from the R. Gardon in spate by a tall dike, *Anduze* has stood at the gateway to the Cévennes for the past three thousand years. The picturesque town is proud of its pottery workshops which produced the great glazed earthenware vases that decorated the gardens in Versailles as far back as 1680, but it is even more proud of its history. As a Calvinist stronghold from 1557 onwards and the seat of the General Assembly of Protestants in Lower Languedoc (1579), the "Geneva of the Cévennes" resisted all attempts at repression. It was given massive fortifications by the Duc de Rohan and spared during the campaign led by Louis XIII and Richelieu in 1629. It was not

Anduze at the foot of Mount Saint-Julien.

A close-up of a roof.

Anduze, the pagoda-fountain.

until the Edict of Pardon was signed in Alès that same year, that the town decided to lay down its arms and dismantle the fortifications. Nowadays, only the old clocktower is still standing. However, Anduze has a fine 17th-century mansion, a music museum housing 1,400 instruments, a strange fountain with a roof in the shape of a pagoda, an old covered market,

The bamboos in the Prafrance Park.

and some very attractive, winding, narrow streets.

One mile from the town is the *Prafrance Park,* an amazing and bewildering spectacle that seems to be part of a fantasy world. Because of a localised and exceptionally mild climate, there are several hectares of bamboo forest 65 ft. high, Californian redwoods, an arboretum of tropical species, greenhouses and ponds full of lotus flowers. This astonishing park was created c. 1880 by an agronomist named Martel and has been used as a filmset when tropical settings were required.

The Cévennes steam train runs to *Saint-Jean-du-Gard,* a town including the Museum of the Cévennes Valleys that illustrates everyday life in the Cévennes, a veteran and vintage car museum, and the amazing Atlantide Park which has 48 aquariums full of tropical fish.

BEAUCAIRE
AND ITS MEDIAEVAL FAIRS

*B*eaucaire, the rival of Tarascon on the other bank of the R. Rhône, is famous for the fair first organised in 1217. Every year in July, it attracted almost 300,000 visitors — merchants from Flanders who came to sell their cloth, English traders, merchants from Provence selling oil, Oriental traders with their spices, Spaniards, Africans, not to mention the numerous street entertainers who came to liven up the "dusty feet" i.e. the merchants. Each street specialised in

The fortress in Beaucaire.

ber of chambers filled with rock formations — the Conference Hall that can hold six hundred people, the Pot-holers' Camp, the Chamber of Fallen Rocks, and the famous waterfall sparkling with greenish-blue pools. You can also see "cave pearls", strange "disks", pure calcite stalactites, and some astonishing rock formations resembling draped pieces of cloth.

THE GARDON GORGE

If you have visited the Pont de Gard, why not drive a little further to the Gardon Gorge? You could stop in the village of Sanilhac from which a rather dizzy footpath leads to a spur of rock overlooking the Gardon. Up there, you will find the *Baume Cave*. Nearby are a number of places used during the filming of *"The Wages of Fear"*. After Sanilhac, follow the D112 road to Campagnac and the Saint-Nicolas Bridge which marks the start of the footpath running through the gorge to Russan. If you do walk here, though, pay particular attention to sudden rises in the level of the river. The white limestone cliffs riddled with caves rise to heights of 260 ft. in places. Continue to Dions and the Espeluca Abyss whose gaping mouth can be found hidden in the midst of the neighbouring scrub.

Beaucaire. The old town.

one particular trade. There was the Rue du Beaujolais, the Rue des Orfèvres (Goldsmiths) etc. A huge bazaar was held at the foot of the hill below the castle which was built on the orders of Louis IX and demolished by order of Richelieu. The triangular *keep* is still standing, though, and from its terrace there is a magnificent view across the Rhône and the Alpilles.

LA COCALIÈRE CAVE

Almost 22 miles of already-explored galleries, inexplicable shapes, dazzling colours, this is the Cocalière Cave to the north of Alès, the largest cave in France. A gallery three-quarters of a mile long connects a num-

Lodève. St. Fulcran's Church and its impressive Gothic tower.

LODÈVE,
GATEWAY TO
THE LARZAC PLATEAU

Standing at the confluence of the rivers Lergue and Soulondres, the picturesque "drapers" town of Lodève still commemorates St. Fulcran, Bishop from 949 A.D. to 1006, whose body had not suffered any decomposition despite the passing Centuries when, in July 1573, it was chopped to pieces by Calvinist troops. The church, which was restored after the Wars of Religion, is remarkable for its 189-foot Gothic tower, its defensive walls and the rose window in the West Front. The old cloisters (14th-17th Centuries) house an archaeological museum.

Lodève. The summer festival.

The birthplace of Cardinal de Fleury also has a museum of local history, a number of superb 18th-century townhouses in the merchants' district, and a national carpet factory which was an annex of the Gobelins works in Paris. Not far away, the CEA company mines uranium in an open-cast mine at Le Mas d'Alary; it is processed in the plant in Saint-Martin-du-Bosc. Prospecting for the mining industry has revealed fossils of bipede dinosaurs and an aphelosauras that was 280 million years old.

The D35 (Bédarieux direction) and the road running along the banks of the R. Orb lead to *Avène-les-Bains*. The spa town was relaunched in 1987 with the backing of the Laboratoires Pierre Fabre. The Sainte-Odile spring is famous for its soothing effects and the water is used in the treatment of skin diseases and burns.

NÎMES,
THE PEARL OF THE ROMAN EMPIRE

Set up near the sacred spring that can still be seen in the "Jardin de la Fontaine", the original Nemausus was named after a local god and, in the year 19 B.C. in the reign of Caesar Augustus, it became one of the most beautiful and busiest cities in the Narbonnaise region of Roman Gaul and, indeed, in the entire Roman Empire. A colony of Roman legionaries on their way home from Egypt settled here, which explains the crocodile on the town's coat-of-arms. The Domitian Way, which linked Italy and Spain, ran through Nemausus, and six other major roads started from the town.

Seven hills kept watch round about, like the ones in Rome. The town walls, bristling with 90 towers, covered a distance of nearly 4 miles. Two thousand years have passed since that time. The Capitol, Theatre, Circus, Temple of Apollo, Temple of Augustus, and the Plotine Basilica have all disappeared. Yet Nîmes still has the largest concentration of Gallo-Roman buildings anywhere in France.

First and foremost, let us go to the arena; there is not another one in the world in a better state of preservation. It measures 432 ft. in length and 328 ft. in diameter. The 34 tiers of seats connected by wide galleries and staircases could cater for 23,000 spectators who came to see gladiatorial combat, bull-fighting and bear-baiting, chariot races, and nautical entertainments called "naumachie" (there were ponds beneath the ring). In very hot weather, a canopy called a "velum" was spread over the tiers of seats. On the third floor, you can still see the holes which took poles for the canopy. A rectangular pediment on the north side marks the main entrance. The Visigoths in the 5th Century, the Saracens and, finally, mediaeval noblemen turned the arena into a fortress, walling up arcades, building towers, and digging a moat round the outside. In the 13th Century, after the town's capture by Simon de Montfort and its annexation to the Kingdom of France in 1229, the citadel served no useful purpose and was occupied by a crowd of paupers who made it a veritable village in its own right. It was not until the 19th Century that the arena was cleared. Today, famous bull-fights are held there during the Whitsun festivities.

From there, the Boulevard Victor-Hugo or, better still, the narrow streets of Old Nîmes will take you to the famous *Square House* (Maison Carrée) built c. 10 B.C. by Agrippa in honour of Caius and Lucius, the adopted sons of Emperor Augustus known as the "princes of youth". There is nothing square about the house except its name

Nîmes. The Fountain Gardens and Magne Tower.

The "Square House".

— it is 85 ft. high. Standing on a base 9 ft. high and flanked by thirty fluted columns topped with Corinthian capitals, it is shaped like a Greek temple with a peristyle and a closed chamber, the "cella", home of the god. Nowadays, it houses the Museum of Antiquity and contains a gigantic statue of Apollo, the head of a god, a white marble head of the Venus of Nîmes, and Hadrian's Eagle Frieze. The Square House used to stand at one end of the Forum whose arched porticos contained shops and places of entertainment. Over the centuries, it was used as a meeting room, town hall, and convent. It was almost demolished when Colbert had the idea of dismantling it stone by stone and rebuilding it in the park at Versailles! But it was kept in place and remains the best-preserved of all the Roman temples in existence.

The Quai de la Fontaine along the banks of the canal leads to the Mount Cavalier, one of the "seven hills of Nîmes". The gardens were a sacred place because of the spring that flowed through them as well as being a pleasurable place for a stroll for our distant ancestors. When the water level is low (this depends on the rainfall over the Cévennes), you can just pick out the remains of the Roman baths. But the most evocative of all the buildings is the "Temple of Diana" a mysterious vaulted chamber lying half in ruins. Other monuments once decorated the *Jardins de la Fontaine* - a "piscina", a small theatre with nine rows of seats which was discovered in 1854, and the double flight of steps leading to the spring.

Twisting, winding pathways run up to the top of the hill on which stands the *Magne Tower* built at the end of the 1st century B.C. Nobody knows what its original purpose was (perhaps a mausoleum, an altar in honour of Isis, a beacon, or a watchtower?). It used to be approx. 130 ft. high and still has three storeys rising to a height of almost 100 ft. Its base was filled with earth. In the reign of Henri IV, a gardener and treasure-seeker named Traucat cleared the

The Roman arena.

foundations, causing the tower to shake. A flight of 140 steps leads up to a platform from which there is a superb panoramic view of the town, the surrounding scrub, and, on clear days, the Mediterranean Coast.

Let us just mention two more remnants of Roman days — a water tower called the *Castellum divisorium* (near the fortress) which received water from the Pont du Gard aqueduct, and the Arles Gate *or Augustinian Gate* that was once part of the ramparts built in the year 15 B.C. The *Archaeological Museum* is housed in the former Jesuit College. It contains some interesting exhibits relating to everyday life in the days of the Roman Occupation and a fine collection of coinage.

Nîmes became a Christian town in the 3rd Century thanks to the preaching of St. Saturnin and St. Baudile. The second of these saints, who was born in Orléans, was tortured and beheaded. His tomb worked miracles and soon attracted crowds of pilgrims. Unfortunately, the relics have disappeared and the martyr is now remembered only through the name of the church near the Arles Gate. The *cathedral,* which was built in 1096 and almost entirely rebuilt in the 19th Century, is dedicated to another saint called Castor, a member of one of Nîmes' great families, who was ordained Bishop of Apt c. 419 A.D.

The barbarian invasions caused the rapid decline of the town. The Visigoths, who supported the Aryan heresy that denied the divinity of Christ, persecuted the Catholics. In the 13th Century, the people of Nîmes were converted to Catharism and only just avoided being massacred by surrendering to Simon de Montfort without putting up any resistance. In 1389, the Jews who had done much to make local trade prosperous were evicted from the town. In 1532, Nîmes adopted the Protestant religion and found itself at the centre of the religious strife that was marked by nume-

The Pont du Gard.

PONT DU GARD

rous bloody events. All this history is recalled in the *Old Nîmes Museum* (Musée du Vieux-Nîmes) that also has exhibits relating to the region's industries (weaving, wine-growing etc.)

As a town of particular architectural and cultural interest (do not miss the *Art Gallery* or Musée des Beaux Arts), Nîmes boasts a number of other interesting buildings including a Romanesque house (1 Rue de la Madeleine), a Gothic house (11 rue des Marchands), the *fountain* carved by Pradier (1848), the birthplace of the writer *Alphonse Daudet* (20 boulevard Gambetta), and several sumptuous Renaissance or Classical mansions (Rue de la Trésorerie, Rue Dorée).

Beyond the Gardon Gorge is the marvellous, world-famous Roman aqueduct, the Pont du Gard. Built c. 19 B.C. by Agrippa, who was Caesar Augustus' son-in-law, this bridge and the aqueduct beyond it took water from the Eure spring near Uzès to Nîmes. In fact, 20,000 cu. metres of water flowed along a distance of 31 miles every day, down an average incline of 20 inches per mile.

The bridge spanning the river is an impressive affair — three storeys of arches, a maximum length of 874 ft. and a height of 159 ft. Yet more than all else it is its inherent beauty that is most noticeable. Its enormous blocks of stones take on a wonderful golden tinge at sunset. A stroll along the footpaths that lead up to the topmost level, and to the bed of the ancient canal beneath the vaulted roof that kept the water free of impurities is a "must". The visit is not dangerous and it gives you a chance to admire the Romans' perfect mastery of technology.

SAINT-GILLES,
A HARBOUR IN THE COUNTRY

Founded in the 6th century on a ancient hillfort overlooking the Petit-Rhône, and thought to have been the site of the ancient town of Heraclea mentioned by Pliny, the Benedictine monastery of Saint-Gilles soon took the name of a hermit who died here during the days of the Merovingian kings. Legend has it that the Man of God worked numerous miracles, saving a doe that was being pursued by hunters, curing the insane, and reassuring those who were frightened of the dark.

Saint-Gilles, which was once a sea port as well as lying on the two roads from Rome and Santiago de Compostela, became a place of pilgrimage in its own right. In the Middle Ages, people used to say that they

St Giles' Church. A close-up of the portal depicting the Life of Christ.

were "taking the Saint-Gilles road". The town was filled with hustle and bustle. Count Raymond VI of Toulouse (1088-1105) had the title of Count of Saint-Gilles added to his other titles. The Popes, in particular Clement VI (1265-1268) who was born here, heaped privileges galore on the abbey. Decadence followed in the 13th Century, with the assassination of Pierre de Castelnau, legate of

Pope Innocent III. Raymond VI was accused of the crime and, in order to atone for it, had to make honourable amends dressed only his shirt and breeches, before the church doors. The Wars of Religion and the silting up of the harbour finally ruined Saint-Gilles. Today, the village seems to be sleeping in the shade of its marvellous *abbey church* which contains the hermit's tomb.

Little remains of the building begun in the late 11th Century but dating mostly from the period between 1116 and 1209, except for the three wonderful doors in the West Front. Together, they form the largest set of Romanesque carvings in the Mediterranean part of Languedoc. The main theme is the Life of Christ and is an affir-

The church and the "St. Giles' Spiral".

Uzès. The cathedral and the Fenestrelle Tower.

mation of the central Catholic dogma as compared to the Cathar heresy. The huge crypt, which is 162 ft. long and 81 ft. wide, has some outstanding ribbed vaulting; it contains St. Giles' tomb. The church itself has been badly damaged over the years. The vaulting over the nave collapsed during the fire started by the Protestants in 1562. The former Romanesque chancel was destroyed during the French Revolution except for the north staircase in the transept, the famous "Saint-Gilles spiral" which journeymen carvers invariably come and study because it is such a remarkable piece of work.

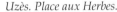

Uzès. Place aux Herbes.

UZÈS, CAPITAL OF A DUCHY

A settlement since time immemorial, embellished by the Romans, the see of a powerful bishopric, fief of the Counts of Toulouse, annexed to the French crown in 1229 and the largest Duchy in France in 1565, the proud cradle of the Gide family now dozes peacefully in the heart of the scrub. Yet its prestigious history is obvious throughout the town.

Three mediaeval towers symbolise the three authorities that dominated Uzès. The 11th-century Bermonde Tower was the fortress belonging to the Bermonds, the Lords of Uzès. It

has been integrated into the outer wall of the Duchy, the Renaissance palace built in the 16th Century by the Crussols, Dukes of Uzès. The front of the castle is said to have been designed by Philibert Delorme. From the terrace on the *Bermonde Tower*, there is a superb view of the town and the outlying scrub. The Bishop's, or Clock, Tower was built in the 12th Century. The *King's Tower*, the smallest of all, is all that remains of the 14th-century royal palace.

The Romanesque St. Théodorit's *Cathedral* was completely devastated by the Protestants in 1563 and rebuilt in the Classical style between 1645 and 1660. However, in the south-west corner of the building, there is a slender round belltower, the *Fenestrelle Tower*, which was built in the traditional style of Italian Romanesque campaniles. Its six cylindrical storeys on a square base reach an overall height of 137 ft. Inside, the spiral staircase is designed in the same way as the "Saint-Gilles spiral". The 17th-century Bishop's Palace to the north of the cathedral has been turned into barracks.

As you wander through the narrow streets or beneath the trees on the esplanades, you will see several fine mansions like the Dampmartin Residence, and you might spare a thought for the dramatist Racine who spent eighteen months in Uzès in 1661. He was then 22 years of age and he is said to have discovered his literary vocation in a bastion of the old ramparts which has since been known as the "Racine Pavilion".

Uzès. The Fenestrelle Tower.

Uzès. The town seen from the top of the Bermonde Tower.

VILLENEUVE-LÈS-AVIGNON, THE TOWN OF CARDINALS

Uzès. The Bermonde Tower.

Villeneuve-lès-Avignon is the twin sister, and rival, of Avignon. It stood at the entrance to the kingdom of France once the king, taking advantage of the Albigensian Crusade, had taken control of the County of Toulouse. On the other bank of the R. Rhône was Provence, which belonged to the Holy Roman Empire. It was Philip the Fair who ordered the building of the tower that bears his name, between 1293 and 1307. It stood at the western end of the Bénezet Bridge (the *"pont d'Avignon"* of the famous song). St. Andrew's Fort was built in the second half of the 14th Century by John the Good and Charles V. Within its walls was the Benedictine abbey founded in the 10th Century in order to house the tomb of St. Casarie. On the terrace are superb Italianate gardens. Other sights include the Carthusian monastery of Le Val de Bénédictin which contains the tomb and recumbent statue of Pope Innocent VI, the church and its famous polychrome ivory statue of the Virgin Mary (14th Century), the Hospice Museum and its Coronation of the Virgin Mary, a work by Enguerrand-Charonton (1453).

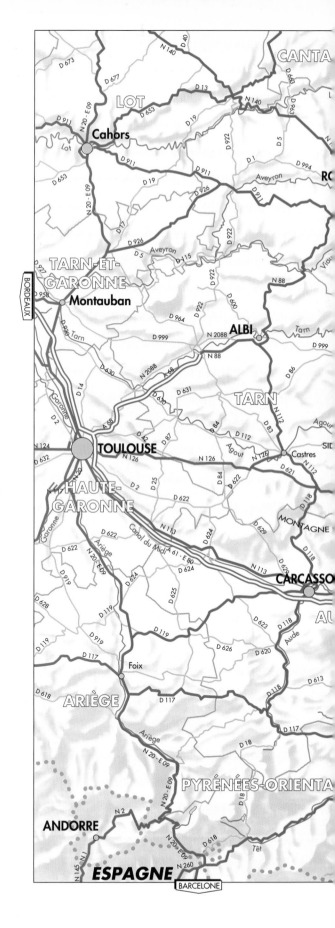

Index

Front cover: *Saint-Martin-du-Canigou (Pyrénées Orientales).*

Back cover: *Sète. The Hérault Canal.*

Cartography by: ACTUAL

Cet ouvrage a été achevé d'imprimer par l'imprimerie Pollina à Luçon (85) - n° 69887 - A
I.S.B.N. 2.7373.2127.1 - Dépôt légal : juin 1996
N° d'éditeur : 3514.01.03.06.96